Bookie bares it all: straight from the he[...] to and for the single, marriage-ready [...] on all sides by the brutal, never-endir[...] expectations. Is it a crime to not be ma[...] woman ever be happy? What if Mr Right never comes knocking at the door of your heart? You'll find answers to all of these and more in *Happily Whenever After*. A must-read for all single ladies.

—Mobolaji Banjo, Lead Therapist at Hearttitude eCounseling

Happily Whenever After has blessed me beyond measure! It infused laughter with penetrating questions and exercises that disarmed me in each chapter. I believed that by my early 30s, I'd be married with at least one child, have a great career, be financially ahead, and be able to retire early. Years later, I've accomplished my goals except I never married nor had children. However, I am happier than I ever thought I could be and I didn't become the dreaded cat lady!

Precious single sisters, read this book. Let each rich chapter bring you growth and encouragement as it did for me. Allow God to remind you again and again, "I LOVE YOU"!

—Vickie Mitchell, Principal Architect and Engineer

In a world where it is so easy to get lost in one's emotional, societal, and inner circle pressures, this timely masterpiece helps singles navigate their best life. Non-judgemental and gracious, the author invites you to have a heart conversation on what happily ever after may look like for you. She takes a fresh look at biblical truth for guidance and relevance for the single's journey. Her take on this much-needed conversation is candid, transparent, hands-on, kind, and humorous. Truly one of the best books on singleness I have read.

—Pastor Denise Munroe, Embassy Family Life

Wow! This book brought tears to my eyes. Single ladies, you will feel understood and validated. It expresses the trauma that is so hard to put into words. You will leave empowered to deal with the overwhelm that comes from everyone proffering solutions for a "problem" that they don't understand. I'm confident this book will heal many hearts.

As a counsellor, this book equipped me to walk alongside singles in a way that respects and values them. In a culture that has hurt ladies without knowing it, *Happily Whenever After* helps us understand our impact and how to do things differently.

—**Modupe Ehirim, Founder & Lead Counsellor at The Right Fit Marriage Academy**

"Why should I live my life fantasizing about being walked down the aisle and called Mrs A?" "Why should my success be determined mainly by my ability (or otherwise) to attract a man?" "Why should younger relatives' weddings make me feel pressure to lie that I'm dating or avoid the wedding?" These are tough piercing bones *Happily Whenever After* set out to pick with all of us. And I must admit that Bookie Adekanye not only chewed these bones, she crushed them!

—**Kingsley Obom-Egbulem, Behaviour Change Communication Expert**

I laughed and cried. Witty, original, and very authentic, this book breaks labels and biases, challenging how we have been socialized about marriage and our life journey as women. Whether you are single or married, *Happy Whenever After* is a book that every woman should own – and so should the men who love them.

—**Enobong Etuk, CEO of Boldoz Bookstore**

In a compelling and bold manner, Bookie Adekanye addresses pertinent and real issues that are peculiar to mature single ladies, not only within the African space but also from the context of spirituality. She brings into the open complexities that we subtly sweep under the carpet, playing the ostrich, and realities that we hide by muttering "spiritually correct" phrases.

To read this book is to find liberation, comfort, courage, and joy to be all you have been destined to be while single. Your happily ever after is right there in your hands. Live it!

—**Bisi Adebayo, Marriage Counsellor, Life Coach, and Founder, Bisi Adebayo Networking Gems (BANG)**

HAPPILY
Whenever
AFTER

BOOKIE ADEKANYE

ISBN 13: 978-1-59452-734-0
ISBN: 1-59452-734-2

Published by Oasis International Ltd.

Oasis International is a ministry devoted to growing discipleship through publishing African voices.

- We *engage* Africa's most influential, most relevant, and best communicators for the sake of the gospel.
- We *cultivate* local and global partnerships in order to publish and distribute high-quality books and Bibles.
- We *create* contextual content that meets the specific needs of Africa, has the power to transform individuals and societies, and gives the church in Africa a global voice.

Oasis is: *Satisfying Africa's Thirst for God's Word.* For more information, go to oasisinternational.com.

Cover design: Marc Whitaker
Cover photo: ShareWord Global Canada
Interior design: Lindie Nel

Printed in India.

22 23 24 25 26 27 28 29 30 31 BPI 10 9 8 7 6 5 4 3 2 1

Happily Whenever After

TO ALL THE BEAUTIFUL DAUGHTERS OF GOD AROUND THE WORLD WHO CONTINUE TO HOLD FIRM TO THEIR IDENTITY IN CHRIST, UNDEFINED AND UNDETERRED BY SOCIETY'S LABELS, STIGMAS, LIMITATIONS, AND STEREOTYPES. YOU ARE GOD'S RISING STAR. HIS GLORIOUS LIGHT WILL SHINE THROUGH YOU.

Help, I Am Single!

Nigeria has a rich party culture. Friends, family, and even strangers gather to celebrate carnival-style at birthday parties, weddings, child naming, or funerals. Most Saturdays in my 20s, I attended wedding parties for friends, cousins, acquaintances, and colleagues. I had the time of my life, never giving serious thoughts to having one myself.

Of course, you really can't be at a wedding party as a single lady without being reminded by everyone present, "You are next!" People can't wait for the next party. Since you've partaken of other people's feasts, there is an unwritten code that obligates you to convene one yourself.

This reminds me of a story I read online about a young lady who was tired of being told "you are next" by aunts and relatives at every family wedding. She devised a way to get back at them. At a funeral ceremony of a relative, with a mischievous smile, she nudged the same set of aunties and said, "You are next."

WHEN WILL I BE NEXT?

You bet they got the message!

Warning: don't try this at home. You can be sure a town meeting would be called in your name to denounce this *never-seen-before* kind of behaviour. Expect to be taken to every known prayer house to expel the demons in you that are making you wish death on your relatives!

Now, at over 40 years and still unmarried, the questions have gotten old. "Why am I still single? When will I be next?" Well, I wish I knew.

If this sounds like your story, this book is for you.

THE STRUGGLE IS REAL

As mature single ladies, especially in our African contexts, we often struggle to keep our heads high amidst a pool of stigma and labels. Sometimes it seems like society tells us that we should not succeed or pursue the dreams God has placed in our hearts. Maybe we defy all the naysayers and succeed. But we have to fight more than necessary to protect our territory.

"What does it matter if you gain the whole world and are still *husband-less*?" they say. It might seem like the Scripture in Matthew 6:33 that says, "Seek ye first the kingdom of God, and his righteousness; and all these things shall be added unto you" (KJV) reads differently in the *African Single Lady's Version* as "Seek ye first a husband and marriage, and all other things shall be added unto you." And so, a lady without a husband is treated as a third-class citizen.

I have been treated as a third-class citizen a couple of times, and I'm sure you might have had similar experiences. As a result, many of us have started to see ourselves as though something is wrong with us. We battle feelings of rejection, low self-worth, and anger. I've known lonely nights and isolated myself to escape the nagging of family and friends. I've been desperate enough to want to hop on the next bus just to attain the status of a "Mrs".

Maybe, like me, you had a list of potential chief bridesmaids from the time you were a little girl. You'd promised to be in each other's wedding trains, depending on who married first. But now the last person on your list has married, and you are chief bridesmaid-less!

Sometimes we can't wait to be married so that our lives can finally begin. Didn't they say when you settle down with a family you finally have peace of mind? Maybe you just want someone to share your life and plan your future with. You long for the security and stability it seems that only marriage and family can give. You worry, *What if I'm alone forever?*

I want everything that comes with marriage: a doting husband, happy children, respect in my family, church, workplace and, oh, did I mention, plenty of sex? That's right, hormones don't respect your marital status, especially at the turn of the month when the ovaries get all excited, ready to kick-start the baby-making process. Let's face it, the Lord will not warm my bed at night! I want to have children of my own, but I'm at the age where women's biological clocks start to work overtime and menopause approaches at the speed of light.

Sometimes we're just so tired of this life. Why can't things be different?

I've been so discouraged at times. But guess what? I believe it's possible to be and to have the best of everything God wants for you right where you are as a single lady. I'm not saying that like the polite but out-of-touch well-wishers. This is coming from your girl in the trenches, and it's true.

In my journey trying to make sense of the single life, I was itching to find out: Is there a place for single ladies in God's plans?

Most churches and religious gatherings haven't often given the impression that single ladies are significant. I've tried to attend fellowships for singles, but I've lived past the stage of youthfulness that they are structured for. People my age attend marriage and parenting classes – not programmes for single people. And it seems that when mature single ladies gather, the focus is on praying to escape singleness.

I struggled to find people who were talking about the issues that affected us – and I began to realize there were more and more of us. It seems to me as an acute observer that late marriage is on the rise. In the past, people assumed late marriage was only common among career women, but this is no longer the case. However, our cultures still place a very high premium on marriage and often view late marriage as something of a taboo. We should be married – or, even if we don't think so, the calendar, our parents, and our bodies very likely do not share our views!

Living as a mature single lady in an African society is not easy. Our mature single demographic seems invisible. We're left stumbling around, trying to figure out how to handle the peculiarities of the phase of life we're in. We need someone who is walking the same path to empathize with our single experience. It's strange how ladies in this category are seen in an unpleasant light, because I would have married some of them myself if I were a man.

I thought that I'd do something about it, so I started a group that I named "Single, sassy and godly" for ladies 30 years and above. We had sleepovers, hangouts, and venting sessions. We tried to provide emotional support for each other while also doing fun things.

About the same time, I was approached to write the "Diary of a Mature Single Lady" for a group on Facebook. Journaling my own daily experiences and challenges created a new level of awareness of what other single ladies may be passing through. With this series, I was achieving two things – I encouraged other ladies walking in my shoes, and I also tried to enlighten society about the plights of mature single ladies in a culture like ours. I stumbled on some stories of single ladies in the Bible who made an impact. It was quite an eye-opener to discover God used single ladies then, and he still uses us today. Inspired by this discovery and the positive feedback on my Facebook posts, I started a blog using the pseudonym *Hadassah*.

I soon realized that a fictitious character would not do. I needed to be real and vulnerable, so people could relate to my experiences. But I didn't feel qualified to write a book on this subject. I negotiated, "Lord, why don't you wait until I am married? By then, I would have successfully completed this phase and would really have something to talk about." Coincidently, a friend told me how perfect it would be to launch the book at my wedding. Again, this goes to show how we have a mindset that the only success of singlehood is moving out of it.

Finally, I realized that just like the biblical women I'd discovered, my own experience as a single lady might be part of God's grand purpose and a blessing to other people. I now find it a great honour to address a topic that is so important, not only to me, but to millions of other women across the globe.

WHAT TO EXPECT FROM THIS BOOK

If you'd prefer not to remain single but marriage hasn't happened yet, how should you deal with singlehood that has refused to be wished or prayed away? I have tried to be as down-to-earth as possible, offering practical survival tips with a no-holds-barred, laugh-out-loud twist. This book will help you:

- Appreciate your waiting season and see how it all fits into God's purpose for you.
- Rise above society's stigma, handle family pressure, and find a balanced and fulfilled life.
- Overcome loneliness, manage your sexuality, and find joy in community.
- Heal from past scars and find value in yourself.
- Pursue your dreams, invest wisely, and give back to society.

This book is not about how to find a man and get *out* of being single. It is about getting more joy and fulfilment out of your single life. I mean, if I had all the keys, I'd probably be married by now. Working as a counsellor has helped me to understand that people are as different as their names and faces. There are no one-size-fits-all solutions because God works with each of us as individuals. So, I walk side-by-side with you as a co-traveller on this journey of singleness. I share personal

THERE ARE NO ONE-SIZE-FITS-ALL SOLUTIONS.

lessons and experiences and give you tools to find answers for your situation. At the end of each chapter, there are questions to guide you in reflecting on what you've learned and in taking action.

Although this book's primary target is mature single ladies, I was surprised how many readers of the first edition were encouraged while they went through different waiting seasons. Other readers were interested to listen in on our journey as single ladies and go along with us.

I hope the book will also inspire you to enjoy the phase of life you are in NOW, while you pursue your "happily ever after"!

Who Laid Down the Rules?

The evening had kicked off on a good note. It was my church's quarterly bridal shower, an event organized by the women's ministry of the church to celebrate ladies getting married in the coming weeks. We all wore a touch of pink. The mood was light, filled with laughter. The ambience was festive, and we had loads to eat. As tradition required, the brides-to-be had to do a catwalk to the podium before taking their seats and sharing their love stories. I *love* love-stories!

As the evening wound to an end, the event's host rose to give a vote of thanks and introduce the different groups under the women's ministry. I was lost in fantasy, listening from a far-away land when she said something that jolted me back to the present:

"The *princesses* are single ladies aged 30 and above."

My expression dropped in an instant. I was going to be 30 in a couple of months. In that split second, the joy of the entire evening was sucked out of me.

Distraught, I turned to my friend who sat next me, "I am going to be a *princess*!"

"Well, I am a *princess* already!" she replied, unable to offer any comfort.

This re-christening became my rite of passage into the world of a mature single lady. It was on this evening that I came face-to-face with the realization that society would no longer see me the same way. I would now be seen as "a lady who was 30 and still single". It also significantly coloured the way I started to see myself.

OF PRINCESSES AND MANGOES

Princess is a fancy name given to unmarried single ladies who are 30 years and above, especially in church settings. In African contexts, there is no stipulated age at which a woman should be married apart from attaining puberty. However, when a woman has acquired an education or a skill for trade or business, she is expected to settle down and start a family. Considering that the average age for completing university or college education is 21 to 25 years, ladies start getting pressure to bring a suitor home from this age, or earlier for those who don't spend as much time in school.

Beautiful as the appellation *princess* sounds, you can't miss the thinly veiled pity that often comes with it. The name *princess* itself is not bad. When you're a little girl, you daydream about being a Disney princess in a pretty pink dress awaiting Prince Charming. But when 30-something years later you are still waiting for the elusive Prince Charming, you sure don't feel flattered when someone calls you *princess*. Who wants that constant reminder, anyway? The rationale behind the name, I was told, was to remind me that I am a princess of the Most High King, and that makes me very special. "But if a single lady is God's princess, then what is the married lady – God's queen?" I asked tongue-in-cheek. Aren't we all God's daughters and princesses, irrespective of our marital status?

People who don't bear the label may assume it to be harmless, but it often feels different on the receiving end. I once attended a Christian programme where each group took turns to dance to the altar for their thanksgivings: married, widowed, waiting mothers, mature single, aged, etc. When it was time for the *princesses'* thanksgiving, I decided to leave.

Regardless of the organizers' intent, it felt more like a parade of ridicule, and I couldn't go through with it.

When a recently widowed woman had to attend a similar programme, she was aware for the first time of what it must have felt like for the other widows who had had to go through that ritual, year after year. She also shared how, in a bid to console her when her husband passed, people had told her she was now *God's wife*. She began to wonder, how did her identity change so quickly because of the tragedy that had befallen her? Did she suddenly become a different person, in need of a different name because her husband died?

While some labels at least seem to come with good intentions, other labels are far less flattering. On social media, someone once described the older single lady as a mango, high up the tree, while the younger single lady belongs to the cluster of fresh, juicy mangoes within arm's reach. Apparently, the older lady needs to come off her high horse and become a low-hanging fruit to avoid rotting because no one can reach her. Literally speaking, I think the high-hanging mango might hold a higher appeal – or why would people throw sticks and stones at it?

This type of labelling is pervasive in different cultures all over the world. For instance, in Chinese, women who remain unmarried in their late 20s and beyond are referred to as *Sheng-nu* (loosely translated as "left-over ladies").

Old lass, stale goods, proud, hopeless, unrealistic, misfit, third-class citizen: these are some of the labels that have been placed on us. Our world loves to label people by their perceived shortfalls. I once visited a different part of the country where people were nicknamed by their predicament, like "one-eyed man", "lame-boy", or "trying-to-conceive".

Stigmas and labels existed far back in the Bible days: "son of the carpenter", "prodigal son", "Samaritan woman", "woman with the issue of blood". I can't help wondering sometimes – these people, did they have names? Then why weren't they referred to by their names? Even for those whose names we know, we still go ahead and add a tag to them: "Doubting

Thomas" – even though he did eventually believe. "Blind Bartimaeus" – even after Jesus opened his eyes. "Rahab the prostitute" – and we forget that she became a matriarch in the ancestral line of Jesus, our Saviour. It seems that these tags reduce people to the not-so-perfect part of their lives and immortalize them that way, discounting the good in their story.

THE TAX OF BEING SINGLE

There is so much pressure for the mature single lady in societies that place a high premium on marriage. In addition to unflattering labels, we are rated as second- or even third-class citizens and accorded less respect. We face pressure in the workplace, in society, from family, friends, and the religious community. Society is structured in a way that constantly throws reminders of our supposedly unfortunate status at us in interactions in daily life.

It also withholds respect and certain rights from single women. For instance, a much younger married lady is far better regarded than an older unmarried lady. Declaring your status as an *iyawo-ile* (a Yoruba term meaning "a household wife") when you are trying to assert yourself or to protest unfair treatment by a man gives you wiggle room and automatically earns you better treatment.

Even in the larger international scene, there are some disincentives for being single. For example, in my professional work as a travel consultant, I noticed women who are married and have children have a higher chance of getting a travel visa because they have more social and family ties. Sadly, the single lady is seen as having no commitments back home that would ensure she returns after the expiration of her visa. Some Middle Eastern countries also have separate visa rules for women visiting as tourists, requiring they be accompanied by their husband or father.

These shaming labels on the one hand and rewards for marriage on the other hand sometimes condition us to want to conform to society's expectations. Our cultures don't create a place for single women, so they try to push us into the roles they think women are supposed to occupy. To some people, we are a reminder that something is wrong, that the culturally prescribed life progression to marriage isn't happening. Although this happens at the most subconscious level, it threatens people's sense of security to think everything won't happen according to plan. They feel a need to blame us for impeding society's progress or think that if we endure enough teasing, we will shape up and play our role. The rewards given and withheld are meant to encourage people to follow the script. But it seems nobody has taken note that society itself has changed around us.

IS SOCIETY COMPLICIT?

Some of the causes of delayed marriage may not be a lady's inability to measure up to society's standards but rather trends and changes in society itself.

We like to say that marriage and the family are at the core of every culture and society in Africa. Most of our communities are built on patriarchy and systems that assume the woman was made for the man, so it follows that she has no purpose outside of the man. In some cultures, the woman is seen as a property, an acquisition, often given out to the highest bidder or the bravest warrior, as the case may be.

Traditionally, a woman's primary role in ensuring the survival and even immortality of the community was to bear children and continue the family name. Therefore, the pressure for women to marry by a certain age (and shame if they don't) cuts across many cultures from Africa and beyond. Today, many young girls are still married off quickly, so they don't become "overripe" and lose value to potential suitors. Being a single lady of marriageable age is a near tragedy.

Women who remain unmarried by their late 20s and beyond are often seen as embarrassments to their families and believed to be under a spell or curse.

But we need to be cognizant of how things have changed. From my observation, it seems that just about five decades ago, a woman who was not married by about age 22 was considered an old maid. Women who married late were mostly the educated ones who had invested time in pursuing a career while their age-mates were settling down. However, these days, late marriage cuts across economic, social, and professional strata and is no longer exclusive to career women or the elite. Why is this becoming prevalent, not only in cultures that are more permissive, but also in cultures where a very high premium is placed on marriage?

Traditionally, in many of our cultures when a young man was ripe for marriage, his parents went in search of a bride for him. When they found a suitable prospect, both families would come together to facilitate their courtship and, subsequently, marriage. Marriage was a communal affair, so success or failure of such marriages laid more heavily on the family than the individual. The Yoruba have a saying that translates, "It's ok to have a bad husband; it is bad in-laws that should never be had." There were vested interests from the family to ensure it worked, and both parties were expected to be on their best behaviour since they were representing the family. Yoruba *Omoluwabi* culture puts individuals under obligation to uphold the family's values and family name. The older generation mentored younger people to help them transition into adulthood and marriage.

> THE EMPHASIS HAS SHIFTED FROM THE COMMUNITY TO THE INDIVIDUAL.

However, with more individuals moving far away from home to find their own paths and livelihoods, the emphasis has shifted from the community to the individual. Men and women now make their own choices of a marriage partner. Though they may require family approval, they no longer rely solely on their parents' judgement to make the choice for them.

Our expectations have also changed. Agents of globalization such as traditional media, new media, and online access have presented us with new ideals of what marriage should be. They also expose us to romance and sexual expression, leading to an increase of sexual relationships outside marriage. Marriage itself is now passed off as not so important; as such, people's attitudes towards marriage are no longer as orthodox as they once were. Sex and childbearing are some of the key reasons people get married, and both are now very much available outside of marriage. Thus, there is less motivation for some single people to get married.

Economic realities have also affected us. Many people, especially men, feel they need to be financially stable before they marry, but this is very difficult to do with the harsh economic reality of unemployment and underemployment. The cost of living, especially in urban areas, is very high. Since men are getting married later than in times past, it follows that women are also getting married later.

We have also lost the simplicity of modest living. Materialism is on an all-time high, so "financial stability" may now mean attaining a particular standard of living before venturing into marriage, and ladies who have greater exposure may have an expectation or preference for luxury. This means both genders may be more focused on education and career goals.

While in generations past, women were strictly homemakers and got married pretty early, the stark economic realities of recent times have made it nearly impossible for most households to survive on single incomes. So, more women are pursuing education and careers to survive. Moreso, some men are looking for women who support them rather than women who can't contribute to the household's finances and are seen as liabilities. Marriage may no longer seem as urgent as it used to be, at least not until the intending parties both establish some source of income.

Even for those who find a potential partner, the high cost of getting married can discourage them from formalizing the union. Weddings are quite expensive. In a place like Nigeria, we would have up to five ceremonies – an introduction party where members of both families meet for the first time amidst much merrymaking. This is followed by the traditional marriage on a later date when the bride price or dowry is paid, and the lady is officially handed over to her husband's family. Then the couple goes to the registry to formalize their marriage contract. Then another date is set aside for the church ceremony, which is popularly referred to as the *white wedding*. This is usually followed by an elaborate reception.

Also, the bride price and bridal list are expenses most young, up-and-coming people cannot afford as they often run in the millions of *naira*, while in some cultures, the bride price is calculated based on the level of education of the lady. Few people can go against all the pressure and host the kind of ceremony they can afford. Many young people end up just cohabiting until they can afford to formally get married.

We are navigating a lot of cultural shifts that have various effects on families, gender norms, and our societies. We aren't living like people did in previous generations, so the ways we go about getting married have also evolved.

MANAGING PRESSURE FROM SOCIETY

A lot of times, our decisions are based on three things. *How will it look? What will people think? What will people say?* As a result, we subject ourselves to man-made laws that have no basis in the Scriptures. In a bid for acceptance and affirmation, we may find ourselves suppressing certain personality traits that are not in tandem with the culture or our environment. Over time, we've heard people's definition of who we are and what we're supposed to be, and so our intuitive sense of self has been drowned out. This is why it is important for us to be able to respond to pressure correctly, including pressure about getting married. If we succumb to the trends, no matter how good and morally gratifying they seem, we will soon be swept away.

In a play I saw while in secondary school, a lady went to the market to do some shopping. She had money in one hand and a basket in the other, but no idea what she wanted to buy. She stood in the middle of the market, listening to all the traders calling out their wares. They soon realized she was confused, and every one of them managed to convince her that their goods were just what she needed. She ended up with a basket full of things she didn't need and all her money gone.

It's the same with us when we are undecided about how we want to spend the life God has given us and instead listen to every counsel, letting people tell us how best to live our lives. In the end, we are worse off because we've managed to base our lives on every opinion except God's.

We overcome these pressures when we put things in the right perspective. For instance, we must be deliberate not to internalize the notion our environment projects on us that singleness is a sentence to gloom. Otherwise, we'll open our minds to a floodgate of negativity, until we fully believe and accept the falsehood that we cannot be content or fulfilled because we are not married.

There's a popular saying: "What goes into a mind comes out of a life". We must realize that the mind is the ground where the biggest battles will be fought and won. To cut out distractions and live free of pressure, one of the first places to start is to appraise the state of our minds. We need our minds to be renewed to help us know the will of God and what is acceptable to him, instead of merely conforming to the world's patterns (Romans 12:2).

RISE ABOVE PRESSURE BY KNOWING YOUR TRUE IDENTITY.

While we do not seek to offend others, we also know not to be ruled by their whims. Jesus was a non-conformist. He lived strictly by the Word, the Father, and the leading of the Holy Spirit. The Pharisees hated him because he did not live by the accepted norms of the time. The fact was, they were the ones who were backslidden and had replaced God's laws with a set of man-made rules. Not only were they living in sin, they also forced other people to conform to their own standards, which contradicted God's. This really is the danger of trying to live your life by society's standards. If we live to please people, we cannot be approved of by God (Galatians 1:10). We have to make a choice.

We must choose to ask not what other people will say, but what the indwelling Spirit who bears witness within us is saying.

WHAT LABEL DEFINES US?

If we seek to find our identity in our circumstances or even our history, we will very likely line up with society's dictates. The only way we can rise above the pressure is from a standpoint of knowing our true identity. The only person who can give us an accurate picture of who we are is God.

For instance, when we are faced with stigma because we aren't having children the way our cultures expect us to, we can remember that as Christians, our hope for immortality is not in bearing children to carry on the family name. Jesus has given us eternal life already. Our culture may value us more if we are wives or mothers, but Jesus values us just as we are, as his precious daughters, bought by his blood, and adopted into his family. People may think we need a man's love to be a woman, but God has loved us with an everlasting love.

Just listen to what God says about us: "for you are a chosen people. You are royal priests, a holy nation, God's very own possession. As a result, you can show others the goodness of God, for he called you out of the darkness into his wonderful light" (1 Peter 2:9). The psalmist recognized God's working in him and imagined how special he must be in the heart of God. This made him burst into a song of praise: "Thank you for making me so wonderfully complex! Your workmanship is marvellous – how well I know it" (Psalm 139:14). What a statement about our self-worth!

God has called us precious, whole, and beloved. As God defines how we see ourselves, we can rise above people's opinions of us and start to live from our true selves. Reframe your perspective in light of Scripture and trust that God is working out his good and perfect will in your life. His designs for each of us are unique, and we can rest assured that his ways are good.

Our culture's expectations and the labels other people place on us do not define us. Who we really are is not defined by our marital status or what society says, but by what God says about us.

Happily Ever After Starts Here

Reflections

- What are some labels that have been attached to you because of your single status?

_____
_____
_____
_____
_____
_____

- Have you experienced discrimination or disadvantages in the workplace, community, or church because of your singleness?

_____
_____
_____
_____
_____
_____

- How have these affected your perspective of yourself, sense of worth, how you view life, and how you relate with other people?

_____
_____
_____
_____
_____
_____

Exercise: Finding your true identity

- Look up Bible verses about who God says you are. Use the internet to find more verses.

_____

_____

_____

_____

_____

_____

- You might also want to ask your close friends, siblings, or other people who know you well to tell you some things that are unique about you.

_____

_____

_____

_____

_____

_____

- Post one of your favourite verses or responses that reassure you of your identity in God next to your mirror, on your wardrobe, or on the screen saver of your phone or computer.

What the Bible says about how God sees you

> But you are not like that, for you are a chosen people. You are royal priests, a holy nation, God's very own possession. As a result, you can show others the goodness of God, for he called you out of the darkness into his wonderful light (1 Peter 2:9).

Why Am I Still Single?

With all the perks of marriage and the cultural pressure to marry, many people can't understand why we could possibly still be single.

Some years ago, I visited my alma mater. I met a young chap who was in his final year, and we struck up a conversation. When I told him I had graduated from the university 13 years earlier, he said, "I guess you are married?"

"No."

"Divorced?"

"No."

"Widowed?"

"No."

I could read the confusion on his face as he seemed to have come to the end of his list. "I thought being single was also a marital status," I quipped.

"It's just almost impossible to have graduated such a long time ago and still not be married," he said, still looking surprised. "I mean, you are very beautiful, I just can't imagine that you are not married." Coming from a much younger guy, that was flattering. "You must have been a nerd while you were on campus," he mused aloud.

Just like this young man, our situation doesn't fit what people are used to and so they will often try to proffer explanations. Some people have tried to impose on me their "marking schemes" by attempting to answer the question on my behalf. Let's take a closer look at some of these numerous postulations and whether there is any truth in them:

SOCIETY'S STEREOTYPES

Jinxed

Several years back, a work acquaintance recommended that my parents go and "wash my head" (offer oblation to the gods) in the village because, according to him, there's no reason why a lady as pretty and nice as me should still be single. I thought that sounded like a scene out of an Africa Magic movie, and I couldn't help laughing. Some of us have heard these types of lines over and over, especially if you live in a culture that attributes anything that is not easily explainable to witchcraft. Where I'm from, there's a strong belief in "spirit husbands" who are extremely jealous spirits who ward off suitors from their victims, leading to late marriages. Like it is humorously said in Nigeria, when your case seems to defy explanation, it could be that "the sophisticated witches in your village have got your Twitter handle".

I do not in any way want to dismiss the existence of such negative powers. Witchcraft and voodoo do exist, not only in Africa, but also in other cultures. However, even more potent is the authority and power we have in Christ. Rather than glorifying the Devil for stealing or truncating our destiny, we must take our place in faith. No such powers can trump the finished work of deliverance that Christ completed for us!

Too ambitious or proud

A male colleague felt I was competing with him. He jealously predicted that I would rise through the ranks in the company but would never be married. After I had "expired", men would start coming to have a "taste". I simply shook my head at how clueless he was. I had no such lofty ambitions or intentions, at least, not at that time or in that company. I was just busy doing my best at my job.

When I bought a car in my mid-20s, some close relatives disapproved. They thought I would chase men away by owning a car. Well, I would have had to resign from my job because I needed a car for daily sales calls, and the company paid me a mileage allowance for the use of my car.

Later, when my car was giving me grief, someone introduced an elderly and experienced mechanic to help fix it. When I went to pick up the car – which, by the way, was our second meeting – the mechanic told me I needed to really humble myself so that men wouldn't be intimidated by my achievements. There I was with an ailing car on its way out, and that was intimidating?

As single women, we may find we are expected not to be successful, and when we are, we are expected to lay very low so as not to intimidate potential suitors. This mindset is backed up by a proverb that says: "When your yam sprouts, you cover it with your hands". But as my pastor humorously says, "It's because your yam is so small that you can even attempt to cover it with your hands."

If people don't call us ambitious, they may view us as proud, arrogant, and intimidating. People cannot wrap their heads around why it is so hard to find a man since, statistically, the number of males and females around the world is roughly equal. So, it is more convenient to settle with the conclusion that our inability to submit to a man must be the cause of our inability to find a man. It's sad that success and pride are mistaken for the same thing. A person's true character is not revealed by what they have, neither is failure evidence of humility.

Male or female, God created us to be a blessing in whatever endeavour we find ourselves. Like the Church Father Irenaeus put it, "The glory of God is man fully alive". We glorify God when we fully live out of the potential and gifts God put in us, whether male or female, married or single. If we believe our God has abundant resources and a specific call for each of us, we don't need to compete for supposedly limited opportunities or fear that another person's success threatens our own. Moreover, I'm not sure being mediocre is an attractive quality anyone would be looking for in a spouse.

Too picky

Being too picky is the easiest assumption and most popular conclusion arrived at by observers. At my first meeting with a potential business partner, we somehow veered into the subject of marriage. He advised that it was unrealistic to expect to meet a guy who was still single. Apparently, I needed to accept that a "sincere married guy" would help solve my problem of loneliness!

In Africa, a lot of things are premised on fate and predestination, including marriage. It is sometimes said that *choosing* a spouse is like buying an item at a night market where darkness conspires to ensure you cannot verify the quality of your purchase until you get home with it. In other words, getting a good husband is a question of chance, so it's futile to seek the right fit. They say, "Just take a dive! You might get lucky; you might not." As a mature single lady, you are advised to manage your expectations as you really do not have the luxury of picking and choosing, so you should be happy to jump at whatever offer comes your way. You are seen as being unrealistic for wanting to make your marriage decision based on personal preferences and convictions.

I have heard people say all men have the same genes, so don't expect one man to be any different from the other or you'll never be married. Just pick one and be content with your fate. But I believe there are good godly men, just as there are godly women. I also believe that God made you unique with certain traits and qualities that will be a perfect match for a man out there. When we wait patiently and deliberately for God to bring such a man our way, we are not being picky, but putting ourselves forward for a match made by God himself.

Not prayerful enough

My hairdresser once offered to take me to a prayer programme because, according to her, in Pentecostal churches we don't pray enough. It is believed that if those sophisticated witches "have your Twitter handle", you need stronger prayers, the kind that can only be prayed on certain prayer mountains. God is seen as unlikely to answer those *jelenke* (elitist) types who pray in air-conditioned auditoriums! Some people expect us to spend all our time in prayer houses. Concerned friends and family never run out of programmes to recommend. Many single women have been fleeced by false prophets profiting from their desperation.

I have nothing against people praying for a spouse, but I believe it should never be from a place of fear. Jesus says in John 4:21-23: "The time is coming when it will no longer matter whether you worship the Father on this mountain or in Jerusalem . . . But the time is coming – indeed it's here now – when true worshippers will worship the Father in spirit and in truth." For Christians, it no longer matters where we pray; God is Spirit and he always hears his people. Rather than going from one prayer house to another, seeking to be delivered from singleness, we must invest in cultivating a personal relationship with God. When we know God for ourselves, he will reveal his heart and thoughts concerning us, so our prayers will be from a place of understanding, not fear.

Too prudish or too promiscuous

Walking into a bank one morning, I heard someone call out from behind, "Hey, fine girl!" As I turned to find out who it was, the fellow, a brother from church, immediately accused me of not smiling. According to him, even if a complete stranger was catcalling, I should have at least smiled to show that I was friendly and approachable.

YOU JUST CAN'T WIN WITH EVERYBODY.

As a single lady seeking to be hitched, you're expected to "entertain both angels and demons" as you do not know which one could be a potential suitor. What these proponents do not realize is how single ladies are easy targets for people with less-than-noble motives. While we shouldn't live in constant fear of being harmed, we also need to be cautious.

I have also been told that I am too principled, and guys don't really like that. "You have to loosen up and do what guys want so as to get them." Sometimes you are told to compromise on your values in the name of lightening up. You are told, "Go to where the men are, do the things they like, be more flexible, otherwise, you'll die single." Women who follow this advice gradually start to lose who they are and become miserable.

Ironically another school of thought believes the reason why women remain unmarried for longer than necessary is because of their promiscuity. Such women are paying for their past sins. The same people who judge us for not being friendly will subject us to serious scrutiny and criticism if we are deemed to have fallen short of the "good girls' code" or of not being "wife-material" enough. Any misstep is seen as the reason why we are still unmarried!

The truth is, you just can't win with everybody. Some people already prejudge you, no matter how much you try to do right by them. This is not necessarily about you. If you are always adjusting your course according to other people's moral compasses, you will soon find yourself lost. Let your actions be guided by God's Word. Ask him to check your motives and give you wisdom and protection. Then don't worry too much about others' opinions.

Irresponsible or immoral

Some people believe that a person must have a sinister agenda to remain single. Marriage is seen as coming of age, so when people get married, they're told that they have now finally become responsible. Remaining unmarried is often attributed to an attempt to perpetuate vices like philandering or prostituting because getting married is seen as an antidote for such tendencies. I once heard a non-Christian cleric say on the radio that men who marry more than one wife are doing single ladies a favour by helping them not to end up as prostitutes. But not all single people are irresponsible or sleeping around, and marriage does not automatically make a person responsible or sexually faithful.

Unfortunately, because of this belief, some of my now-married friends no longer want to associate with me, worried I might snatch their husbands and become a "side-chick". One of my prayer partners totally cut me off the moment she got engaged because she thought I'd be jealous – perhaps the way she would have felt if the tables were turned. Another friend told me point-blank that she could no longer be my friend after she got married as she felt people would not respect her if she associated with me. Some husbands may not want you around their wives as they think you could be a bad influence on them.

Worst of all, some singles are advised to dissociate from their single friends, as they do not want the "bad luck" to rub off on them. Once, I called a friend to plan how to meet up. In the background, an older colleague was interrogating her to know if I was married because, according to him, she would never get married if she kept mingling with other single ladies.

WE MUST RESIST THESE LIES ABOUT OUR SINGLE STATUS.

These stereotypes say more about society's faulty profiling than they do about the single lady herself. They can be seriously harmful, leaving women vulnerable to exploitation by false prophets, opportunist ladies' men, or sellers of potions and charms. They can cause women to lose their social support, abandon their moral integrity, or stifle their giftings and success. We must resist these lies about our single status.

HOW TO ANSWER THE QUESTION

Over 10 years ago, I was huddled up in the car with some friends and relatives on our way from a cousin's wedding. One of my little cousins, who was then in her early 20s, seriously asked, "Aunty Bookie, so when is your own wedding?" It might not have mattered very much if the question had come from someone else, but it made a lot of difference coming from a younger cousin who had always looked up to me as a role model.

I was caught off guard and stuttered, trying to sound coherent and to make light of a question that had suddenly thrown me in the spotlight in the cruellest way.

"Well, since you don't want to tell us when you're getting married, I just wanted to let you know that I'll be getting married soon."

"Oh, wow! Congratulations, that's so nice." I hope I managed to sound enthusiastic as I hid my own embarrassment. Such a simple and innocent question can be so unsettling and embarrassing for a single lady – especially when you don't have any date in view, and it doesn't look like it's going to happen anytime in the foreseeable future.

Sometimes, instead of filling in the blanks for why we're still single, people ask us to answer for our status:

"When are you getting married?"

"Why are you not married?"

"Don't you plan to get married?"

Believe me, the questions will never stop coming. It's just people's nature to be inquisitive. I know even married and newlywed folks are not spared: "So, when are you having babies?" and "Why are you wasting time?" or "Don't you think it's time for another baby? It's better to finish the baby-business as quickly as possible." It's wise to anticipate and prepare for these questions.

So here are some tips on how you may respond to typical questions around why you're not married or when you plan to get married. Please note these are not auto-responder statements – your responses could also depend on who's asking.

Identify circles of accountability

The first step is to identify who's asking, why, and where they're coming from. One of the ways to manage pressure from people is to understand that you are not accountable to everyone, then go a step further to recognize people to whom you should be accountable.

There are three categories of people we have to deal with in our daily lives:

1) **Stranger.** *Low level accountability*: Another word for this group is *outsider*. They barely know us, and our interactions are limited, surface and sometimes, one-off. They could be neighbours, colleagues or the woman down the street. We don't have to hold ourselves up to their standards because they don't know us enough and are not invested in our lives.

2) **Acquaintance.** *Medium level accountability:* These are familiar people who know us to some extent, but probably not enough. They are not fully invested or their concern is askew; for example, if the only thing they care about in our lives is us getting married. Sometimes, it's people we are actually close to, but their concern is rather veiled rivalry – they are sizing you up to know how you are achieving in comparison to themselves. This group I just described are humorously tagged "monitoring spirits" in the Nigerian lingua. We need to gauge their motives and interest to decide how much access we want to give them into our personal concerns.

3) **Inner circle.** *High level accountability:* These relationships are based on trust and aligned values. They have proven over time to not only be genuinely interested in us but also to understand our journey. They have walked side-by-side with us. They are concerned not just about us being married, but about us being successful in the different aspects of our lives. We give these people the permission to hold us accountable because we have come to trust their motives.

YOU ARE NOT ACCOUNTABLE TO EVERYONE.

These circles can be fluid with people moving in and out. Which circle they are in has nothing to do with how long you've known them or how closely related you are. A sibling or family member could be an acquaintance or outsider, while someone you've met for a short time or are not related to could fall into the inner circle. You don't need to let someone who's an outsider into your business, no matter how entitled they believe they are. Your assessment of their motives, values, and level of investment will determine what circle each person falls into. When you're not sure, you can give a person a chance to prove which of the circles they belong to.

Perhaps it sounds harsh to determine who is in and who is out of your inner circle and respond accordingly. But remember, even Jesus had an inner circle of disciples. He explained to them the meaning of certain parables and prophecies, explained that he was the Messiah, and shared that he would be killed.

For strangers and acquaintances, he responded in many of the ways we described above. He often used questions to expose the motives of the Pharisees when they tested him. He sometimes answered directly or used humour to respond to other people.

We even see Jesus putting distance between himself and people who wanted to pressure him with plans for his life, such as when the crowds wanted to make him king by force after he fed the 5,000. Jesus withdrew to a mountain instead (John 6:15). So be very wise about discerning where people fall in your circles, and then don't feel guilty about setting healthy boundaries.

You may also ask yourself questions to determine which level of accountability they fall into. For instance:

- What's their belief about marriage?
- What's the motive of their concern?
- How vested are they in seeing you are successful in marriage?
- If you were to have issues in marriage, would they be people you could go to?

- Are they just snooping for information or are they genuinely concerned?
- Are they trying to compare you against someone else or highlight a perceived inadequacy?
- How do they perceive you or your worth as an unmarried person?

Learn to differentiate people who are genuinely concerned from those who are simply fishing for stories or who want to pass on their worry bug to you. If you determine that someone is not looking out for you as a whole person, remember that some people can't be influenced to see from a different viewpoint. Be wise in picking your battles, and don't waste energy there.

YOU DON'T OWE EVERYBODY AN EXPLANATION.

More ways to respond

Here are some tips for responding to the million-dollar question:

Confirm motive. There is a saying that Africans answer questions with questions. Sometimes I ask people why they're asking in order to appraise their motives and decide how to respond to them. Some people just want to know where you are in your mind to determine how they can advise and support you. Some people are just being nosy. Of course, it may come across as rude to ask these questions of older people, so be circumspect when you ask.

Don't feel obligated. It's OK to tell strangers and acquaintances in a non-offensive manner that it's your private life and you're not comfortable discussing it. You really don't owe everybody an explanation for not being married, so do not feel obligated to give one. No doubt, some will get offended by this. A famous Nigerian musician, Chief Ebenezer Obey, sang a song based on Aesop's fable which narrates the story of a man, his son, and their donkey taking a trip. Everybody they met on the road had an opinion about who was supposed to ride the donkey. Some said the father, some said the son, and others even said riding the donkey was animal cruelty. In trying to please everyone, they lost the donkey. You can't please everyone!

Sometimes, run. Some people are never going to see it. Perhaps they'd be so miserable if they were in your shoes that they don't see how you could be otherwise. While their question could be coming from a place of genuine concern and love, you don't want to get caught up in their unhealthy way of seeing things.

I had a friend who was in the habit of trying to matchmake me in the most awkward circumstances. I knew her intentions were good; she had gotten married in her mid-30s and met her husband through a mutual friend. Unfortunately, her methods were quite crude. I realized she wasn't going to hear me, so I fled and learned to "socially distance" myself from her. I don't love her any less. But she's going to keep heaping pressure on me to be married, and I decided to not be in that kind of environment. It's OK to create distance from such people. It doesn't mean you hate them; it just means that you can't change how they think. You're safeguarding yourself from unnecessary pressure.

Be honest. Some religious people believe you are not practicing faith when you don't respond in a particular way. A couple of times, I have been at social gatherings hanging out with other Christians. When we've let our hair and our guard down, I often get the question thrown at me: "So why are you not married?" The tone is often accusatory, as if to say, "It's on you. You have no reason to not be married, but you just chose to stay single."

It's easy to get defensive – and I have reacted that way a few times. However, sometimes I decide to tell them honestly that I don't know when I will get married. To this I have been accused of not speaking by faith. They expected that my response would be "soon", to show that I was really trusting God for it to happen. But I believe that among mature believers, I should be able to speak plainly and not in parables. This also will take the pressure off me if the question comes up months down the line and my "faith" has not yet produced obvious results.

Humour is king: When someone is not very invested in your life, their questions can often be quickly deflected with witty jokes. In Nigeria, a common buzz phrase is, "When are we coming to eat rice?" And that's for those who have the good sense of putting it across subtly. Nevertheless, the message is clear. It matters little that rice is the number one staple food, and most people hardly go a day without eating it.

Well, I've learned to see humour in this, so I respond, "Just fix the date and we'll make it happen!" So far it seems to have worked as it usually elicits laughter from the enquirers.

IT'S OK NOT TO HAVE AN ANSWER

When people ask us why we aren't married, the truth is we might not necessarily know the answer. In my own experience, I realized that I was trying to help people make sense of why I was unmarried. I remember attending a fellowship reunion and someone said, "How can a person serve God so much on campus and not be married?" It didn't make sense, and no matter how I tried, it could not make sense. I stopped socializing or attending gatherings of friends, relatives, and acquaintances who had known me from way back.

But isolating myself was a mistake. Sometimes, things won't make sense, and we have to be fine with that so we don't fall into the same folly of Job's friends. In trying to defend God, they became hypocrites. Don't make excuses on God's behalf. Don't be anybody's hero and don't be a victim, either.

My little cousin's question in the car was a turning point for me in feeling the sting of this question. It was also a moment of epiphany as I decided that getting married is neither a competition nor a race. I accepted that it was OK for younger people to go ahead. It gave me the resolve to wait for my own turn. Accept that you are enough, right where you are. Your life is not defined by what you have or do not have but by what God has put in you and who he has made you.

Happily Ever After Starts Here

Reflections

- Jinxed, too ambitious, proud, too picky, too prudish, not prayerful enough, suspiciously promiscuous . . . what assumptions have people made about why you are still single?

_____

_____

_____

_____

_____

_____

- Think of a few examples of situations where family members, church members, friends, or acquaintances have asked why you are not married.

_____

_____

_____

_____

_____

- How did you respond in those situations?

_____

_____

_____

_____

_____

Exercise

- In the space below, list out people or groups of people who fit under each level of accountability: strangers, acquaintances, inner circle.

Level of accountability	Names	Possible responses
Strangers		
Acquaintances		
Inner Circle		

- Looking at the list of possible responses and others you can think of, which ones fit with the different people you have listed? The responses we talked about were exploring motives, using humour, disengaging, being honest, and saying you're not comfortable discussing it.

What the Bible says about still being single

I have observed something else under the sun. The fastest runner doesn't always win the race, and the strongest warrior doesn't always win the battle. The wise sometimes go hungry, and the skilful are not necessarily wealthy. And those who are educated don't always lead successful lives. It is all decided by chance, by being in the right place at the right time (Ecclesiastes 9:11).

Lord, I Need a Man!

It was one of those weeks when everything that could go wrong all went wrong at the same time. The light bulb wouldn't come on, the door handle broke off, and the taps wouldn't run! I ordinarily resent having to fix things around the house. To cap it all off, there were heaps of bills to pick up. I was just tired.

Well, on days like that you want to blame everything that is wrong in your life on the fact that you are not married. So, I decided I was done. I would just go with whomever came along next – anyone, so long as he was born again and could pick up the bills. It seemed like I had been overthinking this marriage thing. Maybe it was not that complicated after all. I knew I had had it with this single business.

One morning, I was led to read Isaiah 62:3-4:

> The Lord will hold you in his hand for all to see –
>   a splendid crown in the hand of God.
> Never again will you be called 'The Forsaken City'
>   or 'The Desolate Land.'
> Your new name will be 'The City of God's Delight'
>   and 'The Bride of God,'
> for the Lord delights in you
>   and will claim you as his bride.

As I began to meditate on this Scripture, it struck me that God can relate with any circumstance of my life, no matter what it is. I felt a fresh sense of reassurance of God's love and his commitment to my cause. I was very grateful for this and started to thank him.

Then from nowhere, a thought interfered with my thanksgiving: "God, I know I am part of your Bride already, but I want to be married to my earthly, flesh-and-blood husband. I hope you are not trying to say that this will be delayed any further!"

My mind was now in conflict over this Scripture. Instead of meditating on it, I tried to blur it out so that, hopefully, I wouldn't hear what I didn't want to hear. It looked like the "fowls of the air" (Luke 8:5 KJV) were trying to steal this word of reassurance from my heart.

Isn't it amazing how our own emotions and thoughts can heap such pressure upon us? Over the years, I have come to realize that what's even more vehement than the pressure from our family, friends, and sundry is the internal pressure we generate from within ourselves. Even if no one around us is telling us we should be married already, it's easy to compare ourselves with others and fall into self-pity. As we attend yet another wedding, it's easy to withdraw into loneliness. So how do we face and overcome these temptations and trials as single ladies?

THE PITFALL OF COMPARISON

On a train one time, I was looking out the window and taking in the scenery. As I looked through the window, I could see a reflection of a cargo train on the other track. It was moving, albeit slowly.

"Why is it that the other train is moving, and we're not?" asked my impatient mind. Then, I turned to look at the moving train. It turned out it was stationary, and we were actually the ones moving. What I had seen from my point of view was an inverse of the real situation . . . a visual illusion!

That's what happens when we keep looking at other people and wonder why they're making progress and we're not. We become disillusioned and are unable to see our own progress. When we compare our life with others' lives, we see things in reverse.

When we start to compare ourselves to others, wishing we had what they have and wondering why them and not us, we are on our way to envy. Trust me, there will be moments when you'll feel more qualified and deserving than a friend, colleague, relative, or acquaintance who seems to have it all together while you are lagging behind. It often starts with a comparison, then regrets and wishful thinking, which quickly escalates into full-blown envy. We have to be careful to nip envy in the bud, so we don't fall into sin. James 4:2-3 says:

> You want what you don't have, so you scheme and kill to get it. You are jealous of what others have, but you can't get it, so you fight and wage war to take it away from them. Yet you don't have what you want because you don't ask God for it. And even when you ask, you don't get it because your motives are all wrong – you want only what will give you pleasure.

What dangerous results envy can lead to! Yet James reminds us to ask God with pure motives. He is the only one who can give us our heart's desires. And he is the one who knows what is best for us.

Instead of comparing yourself with others, celebrate that God made us all unique and different. Recently, I discovered that not only are there no two people on earth with the same fingerprints or palm prints, there are also no two people with the same pattern on their tongues. Why would God spend so much time designing your tongue that is stored away in your mouth almost your entire life? I mean, no one really cares about what your tongue looks like, except perhaps your doctor, and even then, he is not particularly interested in the design. No matter how nice it looks, it's never going to be in vogue!

God created variety within the human species, rather than clones of a single prototype. Unfortunately, a lot of us are swayed by the majority opinion and spend our lives trying to live by the same set of rules – or fads or traditions – as everyone else. Our families, churches, societies, and even education systems try to give one-size-fits-all solutions to any situation.

But theories are formed on certain premises and hold true within certain controlled conditions. The thing about theories is that often they crumble when they collide with reality. So don't waste energy living your life according to others' timetables. We must find out God's unique plans for our individual lives rather than try to fit into other people's moulds or follow the path everyone else seems to be racing past us on.

DON'T WASTE ENERGY LIVING YOUR LIFE ACCORDING TO OTHERS' TIMETABLES.

Don't indulge in self-blame

Sometimes we may ask, "Did I do something to deserve this?" Well, I suppose some of our choices or circumstances could contribute to delayed marriage. For instance, you might be single partially because you live far away from people who share your values or culture. Maybe you are in a career that makes it difficult for you to find a suitable spouse (such as missionary work in a remote area). While these may be contributing factors, we know that God can bring spouses in even the most unexpected and seemingly impossible situations.

It's also possible you might have invested a lot of time early in life in a relationship that fell through. You may have seen the negative experiences of others in marriage. These or other factors could have left you with baggage you need to process, whether fears of men or marriage, or negative patterns in your relationships. Maybe there are areas of self-improvement to work on, such as if you dread socializing or have a habit of not following through on commitments. I will dig deeper into some of these issues in later chapters, and hopefully you can identify if you need to heal in any of these areas.

Even if some of these circumstances sound like yours, we can *never* fully blame ourselves or our pain as the culprits for making us single. Single people are not the only people with issues or brokenness in our pasts. Being married doesn't necessarily mean someone has better credentials or is better behaved. On the other hand, being unmarried is not necessarily because of any sin or failing to make the cut according to God's template. In fact, there is a single lady in the Bible who demonstrates this well. Rebekah was very beautiful and old enough to be married, but she was still unmarried until Abraham's servant came along to seek her hand in marriage for Isaac. Let me spell out her qualities here:

- Beautiful
- Full of virtue
- Diligent
- Humble
- Hospitable

Wait a minute. Doesn't this perfectly fit the profile of the quintessential woman described in Proverbs 31? She's just the kind of woman King Lemuel's mother was praying for her son to marry.

But no man had married her! I couldn't help but wonder: If she was marriage-material and really that beautiful, then why wasn't she married?

I found no other answer to this but divine timing and purpose. God had plans for her to be married to the heir of promise and drafted into the lineage of the Messiah. This also convinced me further that marriage is not always a function of your qualifications. Wise King Solomon said in the Bible:

I have observed something else under the sun. The fastest runner doesn't always win the race, and the strongest warrior doesn't always win the battle. The wise sometimes go hungry, and the skilful are not necessarily wealthy. And those who are educated don't always lead successful lives. It is all decided by chance, by being in the right place at the right time (Ecclesiastes 9:11).

If you look around you, you will agree that there are ladies who seem deserving of being married, and it's surprising that they are not, while some who seem less likely to make it in marriage are happily married.

The fact that a person isn't married or achieving some worthwhile goals at what others think is the right time doesn't mean the person is undeserving of it or has done evil. Being single is not a curse like society has made us believe. It is not punishment for being bad, just as marriage is not a reward for good behaviour. Marriage is a gift from God, an overflow of God's love and grace, not something we get because we deserve or have earned it. As with all gifts, it is the giver's choice to determine whom to give it to; it is definitely not an obligation.

MARRIAGE IS NOT ALWAYS A FUNCTION OF YOUR QUALIFICATIONS.

Embrace gratitude

Often, we focus on the things we don't have, so we can't see the things we have. But rather than brood and moan over your singlehood, you could look closely and find lots of things to be grateful for. Gratitude is the antidote to self-pity, comparison, and envy. Gratitude says, "I have and am enough. God's gifts are good. There is an abundance in God's provision for me."

Gratitude shifts the atmosphere from gloom to joy. Yes, I mean deliberately seeking out the good in a bad situation, that proverbial silver lining. And so, I'm going to share my "gratitude list for the single life". I'm grateful for my single days because:

- I've learned to enjoy my own company.
- It's been a season of self-discovery and becoming a better person.
- I've gone deeper in my intimacy with God.
- I've not been under pressure to jettison my pursuit of purpose in order to pay bills.

BEING SINGLE IS NOT A CURSE LIKE SOCIETY HAS MADE US BELIEVE.

- I've picked up new hobbies and learned new skills.
- I've learned contentment with who I am, what I have, and where I am.
- I've had enough time and examples to learn about marriage and parenting.
- I've learned to manage external pressure and become less of a people pleaser.
- The whole singleness experience has birthed two books, including this one in your hands, and created a platform to be a blessing to people.
- I've had the opportunity to experiment, make mistakes, and learn wisdom from them, without jeopardizing another person's life and stability.

I'd like you to take a cue from this and come up with your own gratitude list. See the positive side of the single life. Embrace gratitude. In what ways are you grateful for the single life?

LONELINESS: THE BANE OF THE SINGLE LIFE

It was Valentine's Day. As I scrolled through my phone contacts' statuses and social media, I couldn't help noticing all the declarations of love. I consoled myself:

"They're all just so showy. I wouldn't put up all that show if it were me!"

"I wonder if they are truly happy in their relationships."

"Perhaps some of them bought their own gifts, just to keep up appearances."

I scoffed.

I tried to convince myself that I am a very private person and don't like the noise and buzz. Valentine's Day is overhyped, just another scheme by some capitalists to rip consumers off. I even started to imagine how I would spend my future Valentine's Day with my husband: a quiet, candlelit, three-course dinner served in the sanctity of your living room, followed by a movie and lights-out.

The thought made me smile.

What I refused to admit was that I kept stealing glances at my phone, hoping it would ring and someone special would declare their undying love to me and beg me to be theirs forever.

I had my eyes fixed on the clock. I wished the day away. It didn't seem in a hurry, so I decided to give myself a take-away treat. Don't I owe it to myself to be happy? The meal was another disappointment: cold and uninspiring. I decided to close early from work. "Traffic will get crazy," I said. At only 8 p.m., I turned off the TV and tucked myself into bed since no one would do it for me. My sigh hit the pillow before my head.

Does this in any way sound familiar to you? Well, you're not alone.

Lonely but not alone

An aunt was sharing with me about a programme for mature singles where she ministers. Participants were invited to discuss the emotions they often felt about being single. Some of the emotions that came up were feeling unappreciated, unaccomplished, unattractive. People described frustration, loneliness, insecurity, and low self-esteem. As my aunt sat taking notes, she couldn't help thinking to herself: "But these are the exact emotions married people feel too!"

It dawned on me that loneliness is not always synonymous with singleness. You may also be surprised to know that these feelings are not exclusive to people in bad marriages! Even people in relatively healthy and happy marriages go through these cycles too. Marriage is not a magic wand that you wave and all your problems vanish – even feelings of loneliness.

These emotions are universal human emotions. Even Jesus felt lonely in the Garden of Gethsemane and when he hung on the cross. Every human being experiences loneliness at some point or another in their lives, irrespective of their circumstances or status. Seeing that loneliness is an evitable experience for most people, how can you avoid being overwhelmed by it?

Enjoy your own company

It is very important to differentiate between loneliness and aloneness. There is nothing wrong with being alone. Having some alone-time is very healthy for an individual's mental, emotional, and spiritual well-being. Irrespective of our personality types or lifestyles, it's important to learn to withdraw into ourselves periodically to reconnect with our inner self and with God. Jesus set a perfect example of this; he often retreated from the crowd to spend time alone with God. Think of people who God used mightily: Abraham, Moses, Jacob, Joshua, Jesus, and John the Baptist. I find it interesting that just prior to their commissionings, they found themselves alone – and in such moments they had life-changing encounters with God.

"*On n'est jamais seul quand on est avec soi-meme*" is a French saying that translates "One is never alone when one is with oneself." Like it or not, you are stuck with yourself for the rest of your life, and there is nothing you can do about that! Don't dread being alone; instead, learn to enjoy and value a good dose of your own company. Learn to love and completely accept yourself. If you can manage being alone – and the pressure loneliness mounts on you – you will make wise decisions instead of giving in to desperation.

Learn the beauty of solitude. When you look around and no one is there, it might be God's way of telling you: "I'm all you need right now." God has said, "I will never fail you. I will never abandon you" (Hebrews 13:5). If we truly believe this Scripture, we'll realize that in the real sense, there's never a time in our lives that we are truly alone.

Create meaningful connections with people

While solitude is a beautiful thing that can build our intimacy with God, we must take care not to slip into isolation. As a mature single lady, it is tempting to withdraw and avoid family gatherings, old school reunions, etc., because of prying eyes. However, we should always be open to showing up, irrespective. Isolation makes us susceptible to depression. We need to realize that we need people.

Sometimes our undoing is that we are too strong and don't want to admit our needs. I am ordinarily a very independent person, but one lesson I have learned is that no matter how well you can do by yourself, there are moments in your life when you can't do it alone. While we don't want to go about with a *needy* disposition, we have to create a balance and know when to ask for help from the right people.

> **ISOLATION MAKES US SUSCEPTIBLE TO DEPRESSION.**

God created us as relational beings and for fellowship. We all need a place where we feel a sense of belonging. Psalm 68:6 says: "God places the lonely in families." This family is not necessarily biological or marital. We are all members of God's universal family. God himself is called the Father of the fatherless. It is a privilege to be a part of the universal body of Christ, interconnected with other Christians who can help us grow in our personal and spiritual lives within a safe environment. I also believe God has a "family" for every human, and we should desire to become a part of that community God has created for us.

Sometimes, one of the ways I know God has not left or forsaken me is the people in my life who manifest God's presence. As I look back, I see that in every critical moment when I was at the verge of a change or accomplishment, God sent one person that gave me that last push I needed to make it through. They took me in for a couple of days, a week, or months. They were there physically to do some heavy lifting for me or make phone calls on my behalf. They gave advice, encouragement, prayers, or just sat with me in silence. They supported me until I felt stronger and more confident to do what I knew I had to do. As singles, we need to be intentional about building relationships with godly and kingdom-minded people so that in our moments of loneliness, we have a community to whom we can reach out.

This was affirmed in my interview with Omotola Fuwunmi, an activist for multiple causes, a business trainer, and a developmental consultant. I was totally amazed at how much she's doing and has achieved in only 36 years. I was curious to hear her secret to success.

She said, "The best gift you can give yourself is people. I've had people at different points to shape me and push me. I am intentional about support groups. I prioritize being active and giving because I know in the future, I will also need help from people. I look out for other people's needs and in return, my own needs are met.

"God has given me the ability to connect people. Whenever I think, 'these two people should be talking', I connect them. On the other hand, I never hold back from asking for help. I lend my strength and outsource my weakness. Therefore, I am able to achieve more.

"You always need people to be voices of reason. Sometimes you need people that can love you while you're on the way to where you are going, without judgment. I believe that if you can develop good friendships, you will never be a stranger wherever you go."

Shortly before the Covid-19 lockdowns, I moved to a new country to start a new life, leaving behind friendships and relationships I had built over the last several decades. One of my biggest prayers has been that God would bring me into my own circle. Being an introvert, and considering that most of my interactions were virtual and I could not step out of the house for weeks, it seemed a very tall order to pray for. One of the most cherished prayers I got from a much younger friend was that God would bring me into a community he has positioned here to support, bless, and give of themselves unconditionally to me. I see that gradually coming to pass. I believe God will plant me amongst people where I will thrive and flourish, and I will also be able to bless them in return. I believe God this is one of the best prayers you can pray for yourself, especially in your season of singlehood.

Finding the right community is essential. Identify a safe environment where you are accepted for who you are and where you can grow. Nothing depletes you more than being with the wrong crowd. One of the worst things is to be amongst people who are like thorns and thistles, which represent turbulent and scathing relationships.

Be selective of the company you keep. Surround yourself with people who see your value as a child of God rather than in your marital status or your circumstances. It is always important to cultivate a circle of people who recognize your unique gifts. It is easy to get so tangled up in pursuing affirmation from people who value our achievements and pedigrees more than they care for us that we neglect those who just love us genuinely for who we are.

I remember when I got the news that a dear younger friend had passed on. I felt a stab in my heart. She was like a sister to me, and I was full of regrets. Why hadn't I paid more attention to our relationship? I knew how badly affected I would be by this event if I let my emotions take their own course, so I decided to approach it in a pragmatic way. I sat down to take account and realized that I had been pursuing more "glamorous" but superficial relationships, to the detriment of the simpler and more genuine ones. I decided to make that a turning point. I would pay attention to the relationships that really matter, relationships that I had neglected.

Practical steps to finding community

Here are some practical steps you can take to consciously make meaningful and healthy connections with other people:

- Join a social or group where you can meet like-minded people – professional associations or community outreaches.
- Join a prayer group or a Bible study group. Find an accountability partner who will help you in your spiritual growth and prod you on your journey.
- Reach out to help others, despite your own needs or limited time. This can include volunteering to serve disadvantaged people in your community.
- Value the relationships in your life, including your family. The problem is, sometimes, we stay focused on what we don't have and lose sight of what we already have.
- Identify people who have qualities you admire, and don't be afraid to reach out to them to mentor you or become friends.
- Strike up conversations with strangers. "A man that hath friends must shew himself friendly" (Proverbs 18:24 KJV). Build social skills with practice.

To thrive in our singleness, we need quality relationships. To become all we're made for, we need to connect with other people and with what God has placed in them. If you don't have this in your life already, with these steps you will soon be on your way to building it.

"If only I were married . . . " Doesn't it seem like that would erase our loneliness and the feeling that our lives are behind other people's? Singleness surely comes with its own challenges. But we can experience the contentment God wants for us even now. We can embrace gratitude and celebrate our unique accomplishments. God has made us for loving relationships, not isolation. We can enjoy our own company, seek out community, and remember God is always with us.

Happily Ever After Starts Here

Reflections

- Has there been a time when you felt that if only you were married, your life would be easier or better? What prompted this feeling?

_____

_____

_____

_____

_____

_____

- Can you think of a time when you felt really lonely?

_____

_____

_____

_____

_____

_____

- What were some helpful and harmful ways you coped with this?

_____

_____

_____

_____

_____

_____

Exercise

Look at the list of practical steps for finding community. Which one would you like to try to expand your social circle?

_____

_____

What the Bible says about being alone

Yet I still belong to you;
    you hold my right hand (Psalm 73:23).

Give Me a Spouse Now!

I had decided that I was going ahead with whomever came along next, and God might as well stay out of this one. Right on time, a dude came along with a similar mission – he was under a lot of pressure from his parents to be married. Did I hear you say, "A match made in heaven"?

Did I even like him? Hmmm . . . I'm not sure, but it didn't matter. I had decided my brain had to go on a break! He had started to show interest, and it was all looking yummy and good (OK fine, it was just OK) until . . . *poof!* He was gone . . . for no reason!

Now, just before you start to draw a conclusion that it must have been some "spirit husband" scaring the suitors away, especially if you are "very African", I need to give you some background.

When I got to university, I knew very little about relationships and I was concerned about navigating my course through the terrain. I prayed a very simple prayer. "Lord, if this person is not the right person for me to marry, let them go somehow, by all means."

I must confess I have regretted that prayer sometimes, but if God never answered any prayers, he sure has answered this one. It seemed God suddenly became very invested in my relationships, and people who looked promising would move on for no reason, it seemed. Only in retrospect, I would see how it was an answered prayer!

The desire for marriage is a legitimate, God-given desire. Some of us are bold enough to own that desire, while others of us won't be caught dead admitting how much we want it. At the same time, we have all seen (or experienced ourselves) how a longing for a spouse can drive people to do reckless things. Desperation is a slippery slope for a lot of single ladies. In this chapter, we will look at how to acknowledge our desires, yet avoid desperation.

DESPERATE MEASURES

Sometimes the pressure mounts to the point where we are nearly ready to blow off all restraint. As much as we show up all smiley at our jobs or churches, making singlehood look very good, there are days when you feel you just can't go on any longer. Often when the exterior looks calm and placid, tumult is seething beneath the surface.

So, at some point in your wait, the previously undesirable can begin to hold an appeal. This can be good or bad. It could be that you are starting to lose your rigidity. Perhaps you will get a new perspective and realize what you really need is already within your reach. In that case, wonderful. However, it could also be the onset of desperation. You decide to settle for what is less than best for you.

Let's look at a few shades of desperation that lead to serious compromise and how to avoid them.

Shun the scarcity mentality

It's so sad that lots of women these days have bought into the lie that there are no good men left in the world. It's tempting to want to go with any man at all who comes along – knight or knave, shining armour or . . . not. However, going with that instinct could end up a disaster.

Let me tell you about two virgin sisters who said, "There are no men left" (Genesis 19:31). They were saving themselves for marriage, but then their fiancés died. They got really desperate.

Their scarcity mentality led them to do the unthinkable. They got their father, Lot, drunk and seduced him so they could have children by him. Guess whom they birthed? The idolatrous enemies of the Israelites: the Moabites and the Ammonites.

This goes to show that what you believe will shape your choices and actions. But was it true that there were no more men? Well, yes, as far as the terrible cities of Sodom and Gomorrah were concerned. God had wiped out everyone in the cities, including their fiancés. But their fiancés scoffed at the Lord's warning, so the sisters probably had no business being with them in the first place.

However, in a stretch of land just further to the south lived their uncle Abraham's clan. These were the people of God. If Lot's daughters had been patient and trusted God, he might have brought them their own men and reintegrated them back into his fold as his covenant people. But their desperate act meant they didn't make it into the lineage of God's own people.

Desperation could drive us to get what we want but, in the process, we lose what we have and who we are. One of the gravest mistakes you can make is caving in to the pressure to marry at all costs.

For instance, a beautiful and extremely intelligent aunt in her early 40s was still single. Then a man appeared out of the blue and claimed God said she was his wife. She agreed to marry him on very unreasonable terms and was cut off from her family. This turned out to be the worst nightmare of her life. She even became suicidal. Thank God for being a God of second chances; she is now happily remarried to a man who

> IT'S TEMPTING TO WANT TO GO WITH ANY MAN AT ALL WHO COMES ALONG.

loves her dearly. I often think of her story and cringe! What if she had waited a little longer? If only she knew what plans God had for her.

Don't play second fiddle

"I always thought I was going to marry you."

"I wanted to marry you, but I thought you didn't like me."

"I told my fiancée if I weren't marrying her, I would be marrying you."

"I wish I had met you earlier."

"If I had seen you in December, I would have asked you to marry me."

These are things I've been told by different guys. The irony is that they were people I had always known and had some level of friendship or association with. At no time did they express any interest in me until they either got married or got into some serious relationship.

I have soon realized that hanging around people like this is the simplest recipe to becoming a side-chick. Yes, it's so tempting to want to have a man in your life – even when he's already taken. Always remind yourself that you're worth too much to be a side dish. If you find yourself in this kind of emotional web, it's time to LET HIM GO! I assure you, it's not going to be easy, but there really is no other way.

Flee from entanglements

As much as I tried, I couldn't be excited for a particular friend who was getting married. "Why can't it be me he's getting married to?" I couldn't let go. I then realized this was the stuff affairs were made of. It wasn't an easy decision, but I had to cut all ties.

In recent times, *entanglement* has become a buzzword for describing relationship situations in which married people end up having an affair or compromising situation (also known as a *situationship*). Undefined relationships leading nowhere will end in ungodly behaviour. Hanging around a person who is married or in a relationship is like standing on a mudslide; it's only a matter of time until you will land in the mud. When you find yourself in such a situation, it's important to have the hard talk about the elephant in the room.

I had to break the stronghold that was building up in my heart. James 4:1-3 became an anchor for me about the evil desires that make us want what we don't have. With pen and paper, I identified the emotions I was dealing with, recognized God's perspective about them, and came up with policies that would help me deal with them going forward. This is what it means to continually guard our hearts as believers.

Don't be anyone's guinea pig

Some people become so desperate that they are willing to be set up with anyone at all, by any aspiring matchmaker who crosses their path.

Each time I've shared my matchmaking experience with anyone, it's always had one of two effects: they double up in laughter until their sides ache or they are stunned in total disbelief.

Don't get me wrong, I don't believe that matchmaking is bad. Both in the biblical times and in the traditional African setting, matchmaking has been a part of the culture. Many successful marriages have been contracted through it. As I wrote in the last chapter, these matchmakers known as *alarena* ("go-in-betweens") play an important social role in the marriage institution culturally to ensure both the courtship and marriage are a success. That includes researching, getting the best match for their wards, counselling, and conflict resolution.

Unfortunately, I think a lot of people do not realize there is a technique to matchmaking. Often, the approach is to just find two single friends and try to slam them together. It doesn't work that way!

Let me digress a little here as I speak to friends, family, and acquaintances who might be interested in facilitating connections between single people.

If your matchmaking approach starts and ends with "ABC and XYZ are both single, hmmm . . . I think they should get married", that is called guinea-pigging. Guess what you're creating? MATCHMAKING WOES! Like the term says, what you should be doing is making a match, and I just checked my thesaurus for synonyms of match: *equal, counterpart, equivalent*.

In the same way you wouldn't shut your eyes and pick shoes from your wardrobe randomly or wear a six-inch heeled shoe on one foot and a flat tennis shoe on another, please don't just shut your eyes and slam people together. Nothing wrong with either shoe, but they have different purposes and serve different occasions. Wearing them together will be a mismatch.

Because of my experience with matchmaking woes, when anyone wants to introduce me to a potential suitor, I have some conversation with them:

"Why do you think I should meet this person?"

"Why do you think we'd make a good fit?"

"What do you know about him, his spiritual life, family life, values, and aspirations?"

If they can't answer these questions satisfactorily, it's a sign that they haven't put a lot of thought into it. I back out because I'm not willing to be anyone's experiment. This might sound like having a sense of entitlement. Some might say, "After all, they're only doing you a favour and no one owes you." But after all the bad experiences I've had, I've decided to be more deliberate and stop wasting my time and the other person's time.

BEING SINGLE SHOULDN'T MAKE YOU ANYBODY'S GUINEA PIG!

I used to be uncomfortable doing this, not wanting to come across as arrogant, but I realized this approach also helps the would-be matchmaker to get a new perspective.

She or he begins to understand what responsibilities come with being an *alarena*. It's not just about coming to eat rice or wearing *aso-ebi* (literally "family cloth", a type of uniform worn by wedding guests). The wannabe matchmakers need to be more invested in the process and the work it entails or else not venture into it at all.

People must realize that marriage is sacred before God. There's a reason why, during a wedding ceremony, the officiating minister asks, "If anyone knows a reason why these ones should not be joined in holy matrimony, speak now or forever hold your peace." That is usually the most solemn part of a ceremony. We are all responsible to play our roles in ensuring that marriages around us work. If we cannot be the reason why a marriage will work, at least we also shouldn't be a part of the architecture for a faulty marriage.

So, don't be under any pressure to be matched with someone by people who hardly know you and are only too eager to marry you off. If anyone tries to set you up with someone you don't know, you don't necessarily need to turn it down, but be comfortable with asking questions. This will help you decide to go ahead and meet the person or not. Being single shouldn't make you anybody's guinea pig! We cannot afford to keep experimenting with our lives.

Be open-minded

When we were younger, perhaps in our teenage years or early 20s, a lot of us didn't set out to find marriage partners, but in the process of interacting with course mates, colleagues, and other people, some found their spouses. We, however, got to a stage where we believed it was time to be married, and then a mind shift happened. We became so marriage-conscious that we were no longer seeking platonic relationships. We saw every interaction with the opposite gender as potentially leading to marriage.

As a result, we started to compose ourselves in a certain way that we believed might be the best way to attract a mate. We couldn't quite be ourselves and just enjoy others' company, male or female, in a way that would lead to getting to know one another better. In this way, we unconsciously put a barrier between ourselves and the people we are targeting as potential mates. People are usually attracted to and want to be with a person they feel a connection with. However, that barrier we have put up makes the connection more difficult and might project us as being superficial or desperate.

Unfortunately, people can sense desperation, and it may actually drive men away if it seems the only reason you want to get to know them is to marry them. On the other hand, some men who sense that desperation could take advantage of you, using marriage as a bait when they have no intention of following through.

This is in no way suggesting that we should not make an effort to present ourselves properly, but rather a reminder that when most married people met their spouses, they didn't wake up in the morning deciding they would meet their spouses that day. It usually would have happened more naturally. So, rather than focusing only on marriage as the reason to meet people, be invested in building platonic relationships too. Marriage could happen from them, which would be a natural progression.

Don't get caught up in sentiments

"His family likes me." "I'm not getting younger." "What will people say?" Sometimes, we get into relationships for the wrong reasons. Believe me, I should know. I dated someone because I fell in love with his childhood picture. I stuck around with another guy when I knew it was going nowhere . . . because I really liked his seven-year-old nephew. Crazy, I know!

Of all the reasons why people get married, falling in love is the most popular: "I love him and he loves me – what more do we need?" We get caught up in the mushiness of the moment and forget to wear our thinking caps.

While love is *sine qua non* for marriage, it is still not a sufficient condition on its own. It is an essential requirement, but not the only one. Think about it: most couples who opt for marriage are no doubt in love, but if love were enough to sustain a marriage, we would see fewer failed marriages around us.

You may ask, "What is the purpose of marriage if not to love and be loved?" Well, I believe marriage should not become an end in itself but rather, a means to an end, which should be serving God's purposes.

> *IF LOVE WERE ENOUGH TO SUSTAIN A MARRIAGE, WE WOULD SEE FEWER FAILED MARRIAGES AROUND US.*

This is why, as Christians, our main requirement in a spouse is someone who is building the marriage on the same foundation. 2 Corinthians 6:14 says not to be unequally yoked with unbelievers. I just read up on the meaning of unequally yoked:

> A yoke is a wooden bar that joins two oxen to each other and to the burden they pull. An "unequally yoked" team has one stronger ox and one weaker, or one taller and one shorter. The weaker or shorter ox would walk more slowly than the taller, stronger one, causing the load to go around in circles. When oxen are unequally yoked, they cannot perform the task set before them. Instead of working together, they are at odds with one another.[1]

Marriage is very important in God's agenda and discovering the purpose of marriage is central to the fulfilment of our purpose in God. Unfortunately for some, marriage becomes an obstacle rather than a vehicle for pursuing God's purposes. If we're serious about following after God, why would we choose to link up with someone who will pull us back? Let's choose our battles wisely.

---

1   "What does it mean to be unequally yoked?" GotQuestions.org, 4 February 2022, https://www.gotquestions.org/unequally-yoked.html.

While Paul was not speaking in the context of relationship with other believers in 2 Corinthians 6:14, I think we can apply a similar principle to believers when they don't have the same vision, focus, and destination. Marriage is partnership. Marriages are more likely to survive and thrive if the partners have shared vision and assignment going for them. Having our life's purpose or vocation as a common ground is very likely a plus for the marriage. When we are deliberate about whom we choose to spend our time and lives with, then we will have relationships that complement our goals and life purpose rather than compete with them.

Differentiate between faith and desperation

Sometimes desperation takes on a spiritual tone. I was once at a programme where singles were asked to pick a wedding date within three months in faith. I queried that logic, "What happened to courtship, going through premarital counselling, and accountability?" I was told my questions reeked of a lack of faith.

Fine, I do not dispute that such miracles could happen. Nor do I think that the success of a marriage is a direct product of the length of the courtship. Picking a date may have even worked for a few people in the past. But I see that sometimes those seeming acts of faith are born out of desperation.

Marriage is God's idea, and we must be willing to do it his way, rather than go with our whims. Whom we marry will, to a very large extent, determine the course of our lives; as such, we must wait patiently and let God lead us in our choice of a marriage partner.

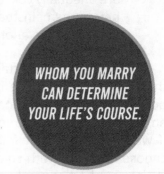

WHOM YOU MARRY CAN DETERMINE YOUR LIFE'S COURSE.

WHY DO YOU WANT TO GET MARRIED?

Desperation is what happens when our desires spiral out of control. What is a healthier response? I think the first step is to acknowledge our desire to be married. The second is to examine our motives for desiring to be married.

So, why do you want to get married?

This question sounds almost silly. Shouldn't it go without saying? The answers seem rather obvious. But have you ever stopped to ask yourself why *you* really want to get married?

Right or wrong, here are some common reasons why most people want to get married:

Bucket list. From childhood, we grow up knowing marriage is something on a girl's bucket list, more or less. In our cultures, it's the normal thing to do. Marriage is seen as something we have to tick off our list. It is presented as an achievement or a laurel which gives a woman a sense of completion. It's as if a woman should feel less than fulfilled until she attains it, and without it, her sense of self and worth should be eroded.

Companionship. There are just some times when you don't want to figure things out, not because you can't, but you just don't feel like doing the little things by yourself. Sometimes you just want someone to call and burden with those silly things; let them go figure it out while you rest your pretty head.

The value of companionship is in both big and small things – like shared moments, tasks, laughter, banter, and memories. Holding each other accountable, setting goals together, building a life together. Sharing hobbies, travelling, having someone to come home to at the end of the day, and eventually, someone to grow old with. Those are the joys of companionship, and they are a very valid, fundamental need of every human.

Security. Every woman wants stability in her life, assurance that she will be safe and cared for. We imagine a life where someone would pay the bills when they are due, hold us when we're afraid, listen to our thoughts, and fix things when they go wrong. Wouldn't it be nice to have a companion, friend, lover, ATM (Any-Time-Money), handyman, caretaker, advisor – all in one? This ideal fulfils a woman like nothing else does, so most women will give anything to attain to this station of stability. Usually this is expected to come with marriage, and outside of that, we sense a void, whether real or imagined. It's so convenient for us to associate whatever is not working in our lives with being single!

Sexual needs. Yes, single ladies still have hormones and sexual desires. In fact, I'm yet to find an unmarried person who doesn't want sex, and trust me, I know quite a number of them. What's worse is that our world today tempts us with more sexual stimulation than at any time since creation. Some of us would give anything to have legitimate sex. The struggle is real for every unmarried person out there, especially if you want to honour God with your body.

Wanting a family. Sometimes you just look back at your life and start to think about what could have been. When you find yourself amidst friends and colleagues who have gone on to have families of their own, you see how different your life is compared to theirs. They have spouses to go home to at the end of the day. Their children would have been age-mates and friends with yours if you had started a family at the same time, but now these children are already in kindergarten, elementary, high school, or even college, as the case may be! You start to wish you had your own family, that things had been different for you. While you are not necessarily jealous of what they have achieved, it's a feeling you can hardly shake off.

The ticking clock. There's a tactless saying that "a woman's sun sets quickly", often said in the context of childbearing. While being a woman might not count for much in a lot of cultures, motherhood is highly revered. Since giving life to another human is sacred, there's a spiritual connotation to being a mother. Mothers are regarded almost as a special class of deity. So, single ladies with children are ranked higher than the ones without children (this holds true among married ladies too). As a lady, when you consider that your biological clock is ticking and the window of childbearing is gradually closing, it's easy to be concerned. It could mean missing out on both the joy of having your own children and the place it would afford you in the community.

Be discerning

All of these desires are understandable. It's OK to want marriage, and to want it bad! It's nothing to be ashamed of.

Some of these feelings come from the way culture has trained us. Others are legitimate desires God has placed inside us – revealing the real benefits he designed into marriage – that we're simply acknowledging.

In many ways, the desire to be married is a very legit one put in us by God himself. Marriage is God's idea. There is a fulfilment that comes from an intimate and exclusive relationship with another human being. God intends for humans to experience a glimpse of his love through such a wholesome relationship.

And companionship is a valid need. He made it for the benefit and enjoyment of both parties involved. It's a support system and a platform for accountability where a man and a woman can support each other towards fulfilling God's purpose on earth. God also wants us to have good marriages so we can raise godly offspring, biological and otherwise (Malachi 2:15).

At the same time, sometimes God can fulfil what we desire in a marriage – such as companionship, provision, and fulfilment – through other means. Other times, our desires may be unmet – pointing us towards our longing for heaven that won't be fully fulfilled on earth.

IT'S OKAY TO WANT MARRIAGE, AND TO WANT IT BAD!

If we take a close look at life, we must admit that the only security we have is in God. Despite our fantasies of a spouse who fulfils all of our needs for companionship and provision, men are only human. Your spouse wouldn't be in a position to be all this to you, even if he wanted to. Life's circumstances and our fallen world won't allow it. That's why we should have our eyes peeled on God – the only security we can depend on at all times.

When we feel that we don't measure up because we haven't checked marriage off our bucket list or attained the motherhood badge, we need to resist what we are tempted to believe about ourselves as a result. Always remember: our worth and esteem is not in what we can become or do for ourselves, but in what Christ already did for us. To him, we are worthy.

Society has sold us the lie that we can find true meaning and satisfaction in a man or in marriage, but marriage is not a guarantee of happiness. In fact, for some, their experience in marriage has been their worst nightmare. On the other hand, singleness doesn't need to mean gloom and doom. We can only truly find our satisfaction in God.

As glamorous and gratifying as marriage seems, we need to understand that it has to be about God's agenda, not ours. So, we must be deliberate about how and to whom we get married. In the meantime, we can seek to honour God with our lives and trust him for our futures, without letting circumstances drive us to make bad choices.

> **SINGLENESS DOESN'T NEED TO MEAN GLOOM AND DOOM.**

And yes, it's true that we need companionship. We can hardly thrive in isolation. So, it is important to find and be part of a community. We need people who share our interests and values, help us grow spiritually, encourage personal improvement, and offer a safe environment where we can grow and flourish.

While waiting to start our own family, we can decide to make the most of the company God has placed in our lives. Family is not only a spouse and children or even blood relatives. Friends, neighbours, colleagues, nieces, and nephews can bring us joy and fulfilment as well. We can choose to enjoy the relationships God has placed in our lives right now, rather than be miserable about the ones we don't have.

We may not like to admit it, but we have needs and desires. When we acknowledge them, we can ask God to hold our hearts and futures. God has a good purpose for marriage and singleness, and he will provide for our needs and desires, regardless of our marital status.

Trust that God has your best interest in mind

Shortly after my "match made in heaven" went *poof*, I was in church one evening for midweek service. I was very tired; all I could think of was how I was going to get home after the service. My car was at the mechanic's, so I was going to take a long walk to catch a bus home. I wasn't looking forward to that. "Lord, I wish you would provide someone to drop me off at home tonight." That was all the prayer I could mutter.

Over the course of the prayer session, my mind digressed, and I started to whine about losing a suitor. "Lord, why do you keep doing this? Don't you care that I'm feeling hurt?" I went on, bitterly, "Someone comes along, it's all looking good and suddenly he vanishes into thin air." For the first time, I was having a conversation with God on this matter which I had deliberately kept him out of.

I felt God say, "Aw . . . so you miss your car?"

"What?" My eyes popped. I was really wondering what my car had to do with this.

I had rushed into buying the car some months earlier. I did not heed advice and regretted the decision almost immediately. The car was so unreliable I was never sure it would get me to my destination, no matter how short the distance. I had spent almost what it had cost me to acquire it just trying to fix it. It had gone from one mechanic's workshop to another. Each time it came back, it took only about two weeks for it to break down with the same issue.

If I sold it, I wasn't sure I would get half of the value for which I bought it, so I kept investing more and more. Eventually I exhausted my savings trying to fix it, hoping it would get better, too afraid to dispose of it, afraid of having to go without a car.

Then one day, I sat down to do a reality check and decided I was better off without the car. It had really traumatized me! The car was back at the mechanic's at the time. My resolve was high. I didn't even want to see it again, so I wouldn't be tempted to take it back. It was very obviously unserviceable, so I would have it sold off as scrap or even given away. I was ready to cut my losses and move on.

"I definitely do not miss my car! Not in 1,000 years! No, I don't!" I said emphatically.

"Really?" God prodded. "But you are so tired. Imagine if you had your car now. It would at least get you home conveniently and save you some stress."

"OK, God, I don't get it! What are you driving at? I am certain that I am 1,000 times better without that car," I replied with all frankness.

"The way you want out of this car and believe that being without a car at this point is far better is the same experience some people have in marriage. They rush into marriage, only to realize that the best thing that could happen to them would be to get out of the marriage."

I walked to the bus stop with so much vigour that night. I can't explain where all that energy came from. But I finally got the message from the car analogy: I should never get so desperate that I settle for just anyone. My singleness was better than rushing into a bad marriage! I needed to trust that God's plans were for the best.

Happily Ever After Starts Here

Reflections

- Can you think of a time you were tempted to compromise to have a man in your life?

  _____

  _____

  _____

  _____

- How did you manage this pressure, whether positively or negatively?

  _____

  _____

  _____

  _____

- What lessons did you learn from this experience?

  _____

  _____

  _____

  _____

- If you were faced with the same situation in the future, what would you do differently?

  _____

  _____

  _____

  _____

Exercise

A scarcity mindset believes there is not enough; for instance, "there are no good men" Being grateful reminds us of all the good things there are. Make a "gratitude list for the single life". What are you grateful for about your life and singleness right now?

_____

_____

_____

_____

_____

_____

_____

_____

_____

_____

_____

_____

_____

_____

_____

What the Bible says about managing our desires

Don't worry about anything; instead, pray about everything. Tell God what you need, and thank him for all he has done. Then you will experience God's peace, which exceeds anything we can understand. His peace will guard your hearts and minds as you live in Christ Jesus (Philippians 4:6-7).

5

The Wait

I contacted a friend whom I hadn't heard from for about two years to check on her. Since the last time we communicated, she had gotten married. Her baby was due in a few months. I was so excited at God's faithfulness and how so much had happened for her in such a short time! But as I read the closing line, you would have thought I just saw a ghost. It said, "Finally, my life begins at 40."

I was just about to turn 30 that year, and I definitely did not want to wait another decade for my life to begin! Having to wait until 40 to be married must have been the scariest thing I had heard in my entire life. I could not have imagined I would survive. But here I am!

Now that I have crossed the 40 bar and am looking back, I can't help wondering – how did I make it through over a decade of waiting that seemed so impossible at the time? How do we manage it when we find ourselves having to wait longer than we ever imagined?

I WANT IT NOW!

I've never seen anything as impatient as my microwave oven. It is such a nag!

I put in food to heat while I get busy doing other things. Once the time is up, it starts to whine impatiently.

I guess we are the microwave generation; nobody wants to wait anymore for anything. I am a here-and-now person.

I *hate* to wait! It's like this: if I get to a restaurant and have to wait 10 minutes to be served, I would rather have walked five minutes to nowhere and another five minutes back rather than sit and wait for the entire 10 minutes. I possess a short attention span, get bored easily, and like to get tasks out of the way as quickly as possible while the steam is on. Since waiting has been a consistent pattern in my life, you would have thought by now I would have learned a thing or two about patience in waiting.

"I heard you the first time!" I call out to my microwave. But no, it continues to beep incessantly until I am forced to leave whatever I am doing to attend to it.

Sometimes I wonder if we are like microwaves beeping at God. We want God's attention, and we want it now! God says, "I heard you the first time", but we don't stop until our praying becomes nagging. We feel if we nag God enough then we can force him to do for us what we want, when we want it.

I'm not saying we shouldn't keep praying about our desires for marriage. Of course, we should pour out our hearts to God and pray without ceasing, but there is a difference in our attitude when we have confidence God has heard us.

What we often don't realize when we want something so badly is that God has a plan for us, and it is usually much better than what we can whip up for ourselves. No doubt, it's not always easy. Still, when you know God's plan is for your good, it is much easier to live happily and anxiety-free.

WHEN GOD COMES LATE

A friend was travelling out of town, and she needed me to do something for her on short notice. Not showing up could jeopardize her trip. However, at the time we agreed, I got caught up in work and soon I was running late. My phone was off, so I couldn't reach her to explain.

I tried to imagine her state of mind. Would she be agitated and feel stranded, thinking I might not show up? Or did she know me enough to know that if I said I'd come, then I would?

Do we know God well enough to trust he isn't late, but on his way? Do we trust that "the Lord is good to those who depend on him, to those who search for him. So it is good to wait quietly for salvation from the Lord" (Lamentations 3:25-26)?

As Jesus said, God is not like the unjust judge who needed to be pestered day and night by a widow until he finally gave her justice (Luke 18:1-8). Instead, our God hears our prayers and is willing and generous to act. He is a good Father who knows how to give good gifts to his children (Matthew 7:9-11). In sober retrospect, I realize there is hardly anything I wanted that I did not get, but usually never at the time I wanted it.

DO WE KNOW GOD WELL ENOUGH TO TRUST HE ISN'T LATE, BUT ON HIS WAY?

We may not have a specific promise from God that we will marry. However, we are confident that he is good and will give us good gifts. We know his character and we can trust him. Sometimes God has said "no" to a request, but often he has just said "not yet". That's when we have to wait.

FAITHFUL EXAMPLES

Reading through Genesis 7 and 8 again, I was struck by what a gruelling wait Noah experienced.

First, God asked Noah to build the ark of deliverance. He had to wait for something he couldn't conceive of. He laboured every day, scorned by the whole town. I imagine he was thinking, "Why? Why am I doing this? I don't even know what rain is!" He kept at it anyway.

Then can you imagine being shut up in a musty boat for months, staring at the same faces over and over, enduring the odours of all those animals, without entertainment or socializing? I would have been bored to death! I would have acquired claustrophobia.

Then, after the boat rested, they waited two and half months, then another 40 days, another seven days, and another seven days. And after the dove didn't come back, Noah still waited another two months (!) until the earth was dry and God told him to leave the ark. What manner of man was Noah?

I bet I would have been like the raven, hovering back and forth until it could find dry land. How many of us are like that, preferring to hover back and forth, expending energy, getting agitated and frustrated? We would rather risk getting drowned after having waited so long rather than sit still and wait a little longer. Finally, we settle into the still wet space.

It's interesting how a wait can seem to stretch endlessly; however, in the overall scheme of things, it is just a little pause in our lives. Have you ever been through a horrible experience that was so intense it became the only reality of your life, but when it passed, you couldn't even recall the exact details of the situation? Feelings are fleeting. As soon as we pass through the difficult time, we stop feeling the exact emotions. The joys of the present will eventually supersede the pains of the past. Now, does the absence of the exact feeling or pain discount the fact that we had that experience? Not at all, but with time, the memory is forgotten or at least easier to bear.

Noah wasn't the only person in the Bible who had to wait. Many people received certain promises from God and were reckoned as people of faith when they trusted God was still at work. When God promised Abraham he would become a nation; he had to wait 25 years in faith for Isaac's birth. God gave Joseph dreams that took 13 years to fulfil. The Israelites waited 400 years for deliverance from slavery. Moses waited for 40 years from the time he tried to avenge his fellow Israelites until God called him to be their deliverer. Even when Moses delivered God's message of freedom, their burdens increased, and they had to wait for Pharaoh to change his mind. Then they waited another 40 years before they entered the Promised Land. When David was anointed king, he still had to wait for years in the wilderness, his life in constant jeopardy, until he became king.

In my experience, God gives you a promise so you can stay focused on the blessing despite the challenges you'll face on the journey. Some of us may have received a specific conviction from God that we will be married. Others of us may not know for sure what is on the other side of our wait, but God has given us many promises about his loving faithfulness and his goodness which remind us that we can trust him with our desires for the future and for marriage.

WITH TIME, THE MEMORY IS FORGOTTEN OR EASIER TO BEAR.

God's promise gives us the faith to hold on because we know God cannot lie. Whenever God makes a promise, the burdens of our lives don't necessarily lessen; they often get heavier. But his promise can help you see beyond the troubles along the path to the destination. It encourages you so you don't despair. Hold on, "for our present troubles are small and won't last very long. Yet that produce for us a glory that vastly outweighs them and will last forever!" (2 Corinthians 4:17). There is greater glory ahead. Hallelujah!

THE PROMISE AND THE PROCESS

Time definitely stands still while you are waiting. It can be such a trial.

- Times of illness are times of waiting for God's healing.
- Times of barrenness are times of waiting for conception.
- Times when your supplies run low are times of waiting for God's provision.

We spend a great part of our lives waiting – to leave home, to get a job, to get married, to get a promotion, to have a child . . . so we need to learn to wait. Amid a trying situation, we are waiting for the tide to turn, waiting for God's promise to be fulfilled, waiting for a phase to end and a new one to begin, waiting because we know God is faithful to his words and the storm can't go on forever.

Habakkuk cried out to God in frustration asking, "How long?" God's answer to him is summarized in this verse:

> This vision is for a future time.
> It describes the end, and it *will* be fulfilled.
> If it seems slow in coming, *wait patiently*,
> for it will *surely* take place.
> It will not be delayed (Habakkuk 2:3, emphasis mine).

When God gives a promise, he often speaks in terms of a future time: "Only I can tell you the future before it even happens" (Isaiah 46:10). Of course, that means it's not immediately about to happen, and we will need to wait for it.

While we are eager for the *promise*, God is more interested in the *process*. That is when faith is developed, when we receive a conviction, become confident in what we hope for and assured in what we do not see (Hebrews 11:1). God does not work according to our measurement of time, but rather according to his programme and divine agenda. Like Job who caught a glimpse of a more glorious future, our response must be, "All the days of my appointed time will I wait, till my change come" (Job 14:14 KJV).

GOD DOESN'T WORK ACCORDING TO OUR TIMING.

God is a restorer and a redeemer. When you walk in his purpose and trust his judgement and timing, you will find that your wait is never a waste. I take comfort in the verse that says, "In his kindness God called you to share in his eternal glory by means of Christ Jesus. So after you have suffered a little while, he will restore, support, and strengthen you, and he will place you on a firm foundation" (1 Peter 5:10). Goodness lies hidden in the wait. As we wait, we can experience God's loving presence with us and sustaining us. Our trust in God often grows as we wait. We learn to depend on God, experience his peace and comfort, and discover more of who he is. God is polishing and not punishing us. He has our good at heart.

HOW YOU SPEND YOUR WAIT COUNTS

Looking at the Scriptures, we realize waiting doesn't have to be a horrendous experience. The Israelites were agitated about wanting to return to their homelands, but here was what God had to say to them through the prophet about their continued stay in the land of their captivity. This is my own paraphrase of Jeremiah 29:4-7, 10-11:

> You may be here for much longer than you wish to be, but while here – live full, rich and happy lives. Plant fields and expect harvests. Don't just pass the time being miserable because I have chosen to bless you here, even in this land where you are passing through.

I believe this is the same thing God is saying to everyone who has to go through a period of waiting. Note that I said, "has to go through a period of waiting." By that I mean having to wait, not out of choice or indolence, but rather getting to a point where, having done all you can do and being in right standing with God, nothing seems to be happening.

When you are confronted with no other option than to wait, what should you do? There are just two ways you can approach it: be grumpy and stressed out or positive and willing to enjoy the wait while it lasts.

During my visit to the United Arab Emirates, I stopped at the beach. Beaches are one of my favourite destinations. I had a beautiful time watching people recline and have fun close to nature.

Time flew by. When I got back to the pickup point to catch the tour bus enroute the next tourist site, I saw the bus drive past. I had missed it by a fraction of a minute. I was quite disappointed to have to wait 15 minutes for the next one. I walked back into the park and decided that I'd be more careful and not get carried away again, which also meant I would not be enjoying myself much while I waited.

Just then, I ran into a very friendly lady who happened to be wearing a blouse and pair of jeans that were the same colours as mine. She asked if I could help take pictures. She had this big professional camera and showed me how to zoom. In turn, she took my pictures and taught me how to take better pictures with my camera. I found out that my new friend was Canadian and, like me, she was on an adventure to see the world. It was the most memorable 15 minutes of my stay in Dubai up until that point, as we chatted away like long-lost friends.

JUST BE PREPARED TO ENJOY THE WAIT.

As we approached the pickup point, my bus zoomed by again. This time it didn't matter. I was happy to have another 15 minutes of fun taking pictures while I waited for the next bus.

I learned that how each person interprets his or her waiting period will be a function of their disposition – it could mean a time to unwind and enjoy or a harrowing period of grief and torture.

I passed on what I had learned when my friend was trying to make up her mind about flying with an airline to save cost, which was quite important to her. The snag, however, was an eight-hour wait at the airport between flights. She was wondering what she could be doing during the long wait. I advised her to dream up all the interesting things she could do.

Of course, she could read, write, or watch movies. But she could also find out what restaurants, lounges, shops were available in the airport. Better yet, she could exit the airport and explore her transit destination! By the time I finished giving her advice, I believed she would have a very robust and memorable experience. I ended my advice to her with, "Just be prepared to enjoy the wait."

While you wait, who are you becoming?

A friend of mine called. We had not spoken in months, and I was happy to hear from him. After several minutes of catching up, he finally broke the news.

"Well, they say when you get married, the doors of favour open to you. I want to try that out and see how it goes," he said, announcing his upcoming wedding in his usual odd style.

I was very excited for him that he had finally found his kind of girl after a long search. I reminded him of the conversation we had about three years earlier when he told me how difficult it was for him to find his kind of girl. He is a very kind person and a perfect gentleman, one of the really good people I've met. His set of ideologies, however, makes it difficult for him to fit in easily. He is just different, and I guess that is why we became friends, so I understood what he had meant.

After asking him a bit about the lucky girl, I asked if he thought he would make a good husband for her. I didn't doubt that he would. I also asked what had changed or how he managed to finally find an ideal woman. He said he realized that rather than look for the ideal woman, he had to become an ideal person for someone else. He had taken time preparing for and learning about marriage, asking hard questions and answering them up front, and having very open conversations with his intended. He sounded different and mature.

That conversation left me with a warm feeling. I have to admit that maybe if I had gotten into marriage much earlier, I wouldn't have been ready for it. One of the privileges that marrying later affords us is that we can prepare and not have to learn lessons in retrospect. Most of our friends, peers, and colleagues are already married and raising children; that gives us the advantage of gaining experience second-hand and avoiding certain pitfalls in advance. If we are smart, we will leverage this to help us gain speed and catch on better when we eventually get into the game. Maybe this time is a gift God has given to prepare us for what he has for us so that when we eventually get it, we don't mess it up.

WHEN HOPELESSNESS BECOMES A TOOL TO SELF-PROTECT

Have you ever been in a church service and the pastor makes a prophetic declaration such as, "Within the next seven days, your husband will locate you", or "Before the end of this year, you will be in your husband's house"? Even though you say a loud "Amen", in your mind you are laughing and saying, "Puh-leasssse! I heard that last year and the year before."

Oh, good to know that I'm not alone!

Sometimes we can get tired of waiting and being let down, so we put up defences like cynicism to try to protect ourselves from further disappointment.

Some of us have picked dates in faith, made detailed wedding plans . . . and then the wait! In fact, as I typed this about seven years ago, I had just dug out a copy of a wedding plan I had written in 2007. I had to laugh when I read through it because of how a lot of things on the list are now obsolete, and I am a different person than I was a decade ago. I definitely don't want the same style of wedding I was hoping for back then!

Sometimes, we get tired of waiting and become desperate. Sarah was desperate for God to fulfil his promise that they would have a child. She helped Abraham have a son through her maid rather than continue to wait for God to do it in his ways. After her efforts had backfired, she swung to the other extreme of hopelessness. I imagine, however, that after decades and decades of waiting, hoping, and believing, she was too afraid to hope again for fear of being disappointed. So, she scoffed at the prophecy that she was going to have a baby (Genesis 18:12).

Having waited so long for an answer to a particular prayer and it seems not forthcoming, we often find ourselves resigned and cynical. We embrace hopelessness as a palliative to cushion our disappointment; we even wear it as a badge of honour. Although we still believe God's promises concerning that situation, our anthem becomes *que sera sera*.

The year I turned 29, I had gotten tired of carrying the same prayer point over from year to year. Marriage had been on my prayer list for two years already, but somehow it hadn't happened. I can't remember all my goals for the year, but marriage wasn't one of them. I wasn't going to talk, pray, or even think about marriage! I reckoned it would happen when it would and so I'd just busy myself with worthwhile things like the master's programme I was pursuing and furthering my career.

WAIT ON GOD TO LEAD YOU TO YOUR DESTINATION.

Five days into the new year, I was in church for the annual prayer summit. It had been an intense and awesome spiritual experience, and we had been waiting on God for direction for the coming year. As we lifted up holy hands in prayers, my eyes began to scan through the congregation, looking from face to face.

"Hmmm, that looks like a good husband material," I mused, and then I looked at the ring finger. "Oh, he's married."

This went on to the second, third, and fourth person.

"It looks like all the good guys are married after all," I sighed in resignation.

It was then that I caught myself.

Yikes! Just five days into the year, and there I was husband-hunting in church while I should have been praying. I felt so embarrassed. What was I even thinking? Even though I had resigned myself to hopelessness, in that moment, I let my guard down and my true desires came through.

Hopelessness might make you feel more in control. After all, you can't be disappointed if you have no expectations. But it is sometimes the Devil's plot to shut our eyes from what God has planned for us.

The alternative of following God's guidance is always better. I remember as a child, I hated having to look for anything. Ironically, this meant I was the one who always found anything that was missing. Whenever my parents asked me to go get something and I wasn't sure where to find it, I'd first pause and pray to God to help me find it, then like a person who's being remotely controlled, I'd make a beeline for the item and find it effortlessly. I sometimes think of that to remind myself that when we let God lead us, and we choose to wait on him, he helps us get to our destination effortlessly.

Interestingly, although the word *hope* is often used passively, it is the active ingredient that drives faith, and our faith becomes unproductive when we let go of it.

Hope is a potent force, much more powerful than we think. The Bible categorizes it alongside love, which is described as the greatest of all in 1 Corinthians 13:13. In fact, the Bible says that our hope grows when we suffer and persevere.

> We can rejoice, too, when we run into problems and trials, for we know that they help us develop endurance. And endurance develops strength of character, and character strengthens our confident hope of salvation. And this hope will not lead to disappointment. For we know how dearly God loves us, because he has given us the Holy Spirit to fill our hearts with his love (Romans 5:3-5).

Still, I find the story of Abraham and Sarah encouraging. They waited 25 years after God promised them a son. Yes, they decided to "help" God and stumbled along the way, but I find it striking that Sarah was still described as having faith to conceive a child despite her barrenness (Hebrews 11:11). While we wait, it's possible that we'll stumble, we'll make hasty and desperate decisions, we'll come back looking foolish and might even prolong our wait in the process . . . but God is still faithful. We can put our faith in Abraham's God because he has never lied or failed.

Waiting is hardly easy for anyone, it's natural to want to be in full control of our lives, events, and timelines. However, sometimes God allows us to go through seasons when it seems nothing is happening in our lives or we can't go at the pace we would want. In those moments, all we can do is to trust God, trust that his plans are best, and trust that he will use our wait to birth great things beyond our imagination. Having this mindset will help us choose to be joyful and content instead of hopeless, so we can make the best for the season.

Happily Ever After Starts Here

Reflections

- If you were to compare your wait to the wait a biblical character experienced, who would you choose?

_____

_____

_____

_____

- What does that person's story remind you about who God is?

_____

_____

_____

_____

- Can you think of a time you were afraid to hope again because you had been disappointed so often?

_____

_____

_____

_____

- What lessons have you learned during this waiting season and how have you grown?

_____

_____

_____

_____

Exercise

Start a journal of your waiting season where you can make note of key events, achievements, and growths you have experienced in different areas of your life. Visit this when you need a reminder of reasons to be hopeful about what God is doing in your life.

What the Bible says about waiting

Wait patiently for the Lord.
Be brave and courageous.
Yes, wait patiently for the Lord (Psalm 27:14).

6

Singleness and Wholeness

I have a scar sitting at the centre of my forehead. Initially, I had tried several things to make it fade, with very little result. Now I've had it for more than a decade, and I hardly remember that it exists. I have kind of blurred it out of my consciousness until I no longer see it. I have several other scars on my body. Each one tells a unique story – from the one I got in a life-and-death situation to others I acquired in less dramatic, but nonetheless painful, circumstances. Some have gradually faded out over the years, and I can hardly remember that they are there. Others have remained, stubborn, and unyielding.

Scars are often ugly reminders of not-too-pleasant-experiences we have had somewhere in our past, pains we had to go through by ourselves. They remind us of our human frailty, of yesterday's pain that has become today's memories. Some scars naturally fade over the years while others stay much longer. At the same time, they are signs that we have healed. They tell us how God helped us. Sometimes, we wear our scars as badges of honour because they remind us of how strong we are and how much we have survived.

SCARS ARE SIGNS THAT WE HAVE HEALED.

In the same way, many of us carry emotional scars from painful experiences in the past. Sometimes these scars affect our relationships with others, our ability to trust God, our beliefs about marriage, or our view of men. The unfair weight of hurts, pressure, and discrimination single people face can also test our limits.

The pain and pressure we have been through may have caused us to cave in and crack. In the process, some of us have lost the wholeness God has gifted us with, the very essence of who we really are.

Ironically, the most profound dictionary definition of the word *single* that I found is *whole*. To be single means to be of one part, complete, unsplintered, unfragmented. That is the state that God intends for us to live in.

I believe God's plan is to fully heal and restore the wounds of his precious daughters until we become whole again. "I will give you back your health and heal your wounds," says the Lord. "For you are called an outcast – 'Jerusalem for whom no one cares'" (Jeremiah 30:17). Through this book and especially this chapter, I pray God will help you to recognize any wounds or scars you carry, restore you to wholeness, and give you a new beginning.

THE SOURCES OF WOUNDS

Painful and traumatic experiences

A friend of mine was separated from her family as a child. She was a very brilliant and hard-working lady with tall dreams. However, when she got engaged, it bothered me that in all our conversations, she had nothing good to say about her fiancé. I didn't have a good feeling about it. That marriage turned out to be a nightmare. She was losing her mind. She eventually had to flee as she felt her life was endangered. Her fear of being alone drove her into the arms of the wrong person. It cost her not only her dreams but also her sanity.

Our experiences and what we observe from others' experiences shape our perspective and approach to life. At the core of many beliefs is pain shaped by experience. In extreme cases, some of these experiences have left more than a dent in the core of our being, causing trauma. Many of us have been scarred and built personalities around our trauma. We have scripts running in our subconscious that we're not even aware of. They dictate the trajectory of our belief systems, values, relationships, and how we do life. A lot of us have learned to live with the brokenness, to self-protect, and to arm ourselves with strength so that we will never again be a victim.

Oftentimes, we try to move on without really processing our trauma or loss. We keep carrying baggage around. When we don't heal completely, it affects our ability to live to the fullest. When we don't let go of past hurts, our unforgiveness and bitterness leave us as victims and captives, at the mercy of that experience. This can lead to depression and other mental health issues.

For all of us with painful experiences, I believe God wants to bring us healing. He is our judge for every wrong that has been meted out to us in past relationships by friends, acquaintances, and even society. He himself will provide justice. He can turn our shame into honour. He can heal us completely of past hurts. He can compensate us by bringing new people into our lives who will show us genuine and unconditional love. We will no longer live among relationships that seek to hurt and stifle us like thistles.

Learned mindsets

Sometimes, we have not been personally scarred, but we have learned mindsets from people who are scarred. For instance:

- "Men can't be trusted."
- "People with tainted pasts are damaged goods."

- "People from broken homes can't have successful marriages."
- "You can't trust anyone but yourself."

Some of us have had these types of statements drummed into our ears over and over by people close to us. We need to be careful whom we're listening to because information leads to the inner formation of our core beliefs. Our life experiences and those of others may have defined our perspectives and evolved into what we've tagged as our "truths". These days, truth seems to be what we decide it is and what we're comfortable with. But nothing except the Word of God is truth, "for no one can lay any foundation other than the one we already have – Jesus Christ" (1 Corinthians 3:11).

Believing in anything not rooted in God's truth has very damaging consequences. In the Garden, the Devil deceived Adam and Eve with a promise of what they would become. In the bid to become something more spectacular than what they were, they ended up losing their identity in God.

For those of us who have inherited or formed misleading beliefs, God wants to heal our minds. Throughout Jesus's teaching, we hear him say to the people: "You have heard that it was said . . . but now I say unto you . . ." He was consciously working on a paradigm shift in the minds of the people he spoke to. He rebuked the Pharisees, scribes, and teachers of the law because of the hardness of their hearts. They held on to beliefs rooted in the traditions and philosophies of men rather than the laws of God, which became a stumbling block to them.

God wants us to come out of the place of limiting beliefs. When God gave the promise to Abraham to make him the father of nations, the first instruction was for him to step out of his tent. It limited his horizon. He needed to catch a glimpse of the sky that stretched endlessly and attempt to count the stars, innumerable like the grains of sand at the seashore.

SYMPTOMS OF WOUNDS

If we search deep, we might be surprised to find that we all have some wounds we need to heal from. Many people would rather not go through this exercise. They feel it means something is wrong with them or they are guilty of doing something wrong.

However, wounds are usually not the result of something we did wrong, but rather a pain that was inflicted on us by other people we trusted or in an environment in which we found ourselves. If we realize that we didn't have control over what happened to us or what people did to us, it might be easier to confront these wounds. As you read through the following wounds, I'd like you to be open to allowing God to heal and free you from the pain and shame for the rest of your life.

Fears of intimacy or being let down

I met a jovial and brilliant young lady. Not surprisingly, people took to her very easily and wanted to be her friend. However, while she was bubbly on the outside, she was dealing with severe depression. She was afraid of people getting to know what she considered a messy family history, so she quickly cut off ties when she felt people were trying to get close to her. This self-sabotaging behaviour left her depressed and impeded her from fully evolving into her potential.

Another lady had witnessed the failure of her parents' marriage and how her mother got the short end of the stick. She had unconsciously resolved never to suffer such treatment at the hands of a man. She went on to get married. However, she built her life separately from her husband and never included him in her plans. She never wanted to be vulnerable or

BELIEVING ANYTHING BUT GOD'S TRUTH HAS BAD CONSEQUENCES.

helpless, so she pursued her career, made her own money, and lived very independently of her husband. No matter how much her husband tried, she was unreachable.

Sometimes, like the first woman, we are afraid that if people knew us, they would reject us. Other times, like the second woman, we can be afraid to depend on and trust someone for fear they will let us down.

The fear of getting hurt can be a major roadblock preventing us from having good marriages. Take the example of the electric eel. It was an interesting discovery for me that though electric eels are not born blind, they eventually become blind.[2] Here's how it happens: whenever they come under attack, they produce electricity as a defence mechanism to ward off predators.

Unfortunately, they become paranoid. They charge up their environment with too much electricity, so they keep electrocuting their eyes until they become blind. When they become blind, they get even more suspicious of their environment. The cycle of electrocution and self-inflicted pain continues.

In our lives, too, fear creates blindness. What you're afraid of dominates your focus until you can see nothing else. We perceive everyone as a threat and a predator. We try to protect ourselves. Perhaps we draw away and isolate, so no one hurts us or lets us down. Maybe we hide our true selves so our vulnerable side won't be rejected. Maybe we lash out against others to prevent them from getting too close or taking advantage of us. What happens? People leave us alone.

But in trying to protect ourselves from being hurt by predators, we shut ourselves in and shut God out as well. We end up only hurting ourselves. This is how people have built personalities and lifestyles out of their fears. Unfortunately, we keep falling into the same mistakes or cycles we are afraid of. Fear keeps us from becoming our true selves, from living to our full potential, and enjoying where we are. However,

---

2   "Animals," *SafeElectricity.org*, 4 February 2022, https://eec.electricuniverse .com/new-frontiers/e-adventures/animals/.

vulnerability is a necessary part of an intimate relationship, and it includes the risk of getting hurt. Practicing vulnerability in safe relationships can help us learn to trust again.

Insecurity and feeling unworthy of love

A dear friend of mine was born out of wedlock, and her birth parents left her in the care of some relatives. She didn't realize that the couple who raised her were not biological parents until people who knew her story started to call her a bastard. So, she grew up with this stigma, a deep sense of rejection, and lived all her life searching for love and acceptance.

Her choice of men was bizarre. She got into one bad relationship after another. Even when she had good and promising suitors, she turned them down. When I asked why she chose the men who gave her nothing but grief and pain, her response was, "I need to be with a man who needs me." Her need to be needed drove her into unreasonable relationships and broke her even further.

Another friend had experienced a cycle of broken relationships. "I just want to have a child," she said. Her desperation for a child was a result of her past. At a very young age, she was responsible for other people. The need to have others depend on her had become a major part of her identity. Unconsciously, this had resulted in a void she was trying to fill.

I've seen a common pattern with these ladies. They keep making the wrong choices and perpetuating negative cycles because, subconsciously, their reasons for wanting a relationship are based on faulty principles. They are all lovely women, the type that a blessed son of God would want to be with. However, they are looking for someone to make them feel lovable, needed, and good enough.

This often happens when we have a low view of ourselves. Experiences from our pasts – how people we trusted treated us – have robbed us of our true identity in God. Our past experiences of being treated as unworthy have calcified into our belief systems that good men couldn't love us. These are the roots of some of the bad choices and poor judgements we make, which eventually affect our relationships with other people and dictate the trajectory of our lives.

When Adam and Eve listened to the serpent's lies, they discovered that they were naked and felt shame. But they hid from God, whereas it was God who had the ability to clothe them. Like these lovely women I've mentioned, it's possible to compartmentalize our lives, be fervent Christians, and yet keep God at bay in areas of our greatest need. We're afraid and we don't trust him to be able to give us the love we want. So, we keep fighting and struggling in those areas. We will only find freedom when we step out into the light and let God lovingly clothe us with a new identity.

Bias against men

Listening to my friend talk about men bothered me. Once, she told me about how the guy she was dating was controlling. She ended with, "But, you know, it's not like one has a choice. You just go along with it and live the rest of your life in misery." Another time, she said he was cheating, "But, well, all men cheat, after all."

I've heard another lady say, "I can't run a joint account with my husband because my aunt who did that was fleeced out of her money." Another Spirit-filled, long-serving worker in her church said, "I can't marry a Christian. They are all hypocrites and don't know how to treat a woman."

Many of us have formed prejudices that affect how we relate to men. Often, this is because we have been burned in past relationships or seen other people hurt by men. In my friend's case, she had grown up seeing her father have extramarital affairs and her parents' marriage had been quite toxic. While this model didn't sit well with her, it had made a deep imprint in her mind. She didn't think marriage could be otherwise.

She had also been very invested in a promising, long-term relationship. It ended abruptly, leaving her broken, and she hadn't quite recovered from it. This further reinforced her belief that relationships and marriages were doomed to end in pain. It took a long talk to convince her that it was not normal to be in a relationship where you felt doomed, and you shouldn't expect to end up with a man who cheats. It sounded all new to her.

The truth is that there are good and honourable men around us. I have met quite a number of them. The Bible says God made us (male and female) in his image and affirmed that everything he made was good. While both men and women have sinned and derailed from the original design, the goodness God put in us still shines through.

Sometimes I think we can become like Elijah. He complained to God that he was the only one who had not turned to idolatry, but God let him know that 7,000 others had not bowed the knee to Baal. Elijah's negative experiences clouded his perspective and caused him to exaggerate. While some men might fit into a negative profile, there are definitely still honourable men.

We should be careful not to generalize and degrade all men. Hebrews 12:15 says: "Look after each other so that none of you fails to receive the grace of God. Watch out that no poisonous root of bitterness grows up to trouble you, corrupting many." Hebrews is talking about bitterness between believers, and we can apply it to our relationships as men and women. We have to be careful about our mindset and guard against negative extremes, because they can define our experience and limit our perspective.

Pessimism about marriage

Many of us have been scarred by seeing bad marriages around us, abusive relationships, or marriages that end in divorce, perhaps even the marriages of our parents or other people close to us. With so much negative press about marriages these days, marriage is beginning to look unattractive. The desire for marriage has been stifled by the uncertainty that could come with it. Some singles see this as an incentive to remain as they are; and singleness has become a symbol of stability for them. In reality, we are afraid to take the leap to something new, that does not have to be identical to what we've seen in our pasts.

By my mid-20s, I had seen enough examples of dysfunctional marriages to not be so keen. I figured that I'd just "try it out". If it didn't work, I'd go find life elsewhere. At least I'd have my two kids, a boy and girl. I had it very much figured out! I had subconsciously made an exit plan, while not having even ventured into marriage yet.

MARRIAGE IS GOOD BECAUSE GOD MADE IT SO.

Irrespective of the pictures we daily confront around us, marriage is good because God made it so. If done right, marriage and the process leading up to it are some of the most beautiful things in God's agenda. The only truth is what God says – not what people, our environment, or our experiences have programmed us to believe. God created marriage.

Romans 12:2 brought so much liberation for me, especially in helping to guard myself from unhealthy patterns of thinking: "Don't copy the behaviour and customs of this world, but let God transform you into a new person by *changing the way you think*. Then you will learn to know God's will for you, which is good and pleasing and perfect" (emphasis mine).

We need to clean up our mental space by becoming more aware of scripts running in our minds, and consciously replacing them with God's truth. Like the age-old adage says, "If we shut our eyes so we don't see evil, then we would miss out on good when it comes." Let's not allow sin and our fallen world to make us give up on the great possibilities of marriage within the bandwidth of God's intent.

Proving your self-worth

Sometimes even the experience of being a single woman has made us afraid to let our guard down. Because of stigma and stereotypes, we constantly have to prove our worth. It can be exhausting and embittering.

I shared in chapter one about how as I transitioned into my 30s, I came face-to-face with the reality of being a "mature single lady" and how society might see me as "less than" as a result. This put me under pressure to earn respect another way. I told myself, "I'm not married. So what? I could make a lot of money and become very relevant, then it wouldn't matter that I'm not married."

I became dissatisfied with where I was. I wanted to do and be more. I didn't see a future in my job anymore. The thought of going back to the office the next day would keep me awake all night. I resigned.

I thought I would take some time to unwind, but I didn't take a day of rest before heading out again. But one project after another didn't bring me fulfilment. I worked hard because I was so afraid of failure. I now realize that you can work very hard and still fail. I also stopped socializing, attending weddings, and doing fun things. I ended up unhappy, sick, and still broke.

I had been fighting to be seen as successful despite my single status, but I soon found myself battling my sanity and my health. I had given up what I had for what I was looking for, and it wasn't worth it.

Perhaps the weight of being single in our society has scarred you in some way. As single ladies, some of us can find ourselves overly defensive, living on the edge and having to fight more than necessary to protect our territory, our integrity, and our sanity. We may start to lose touch with that meek and quiet spirit with which the Lord has beautified us. Too easily, we become a caricature of our true selves: angry, vicious, as if we are constantly on a warpath with anything or anyone who seems to threaten our sense of being.

I want to let you know that healing is possible. I learned to extricate myself from stressful relationships and toxic environments. I learned to be less anxious, to trust more, and to depend on others. I began to live more out of my heart than my head. Forced to rest, I practiced contentment.

What's more, my single status is no longer a source of shame for me. I'm able to talk about it freely with others, even writing this book! I've found a greater confidence in who I am and my identity in Christ. Galatians 1:10 reminds us that we don't need to live for others' approval: "Obviously, I'm not trying to win the approval of people, but of God. If pleasing people were my goal, I would not be Christ's servant."

HEALING AND WHOLENESS

A pastor I was close to asked if he could pray for me. He shared how he had given a series of his teachings on marriage to another lady in her late 20s and she got married within months. I could have the same result if I followed through, he said. I did a quick take and told him I honestly wasn't ready. I realized I had negative beliefs about marriage that I needed to address before rushing off to get married. He was trying to help address a problem on the surface, but I knew there was a different issue that I needed to focus on. I'm grateful I recognized my baggage so I could address it and find healing.

In trying to help people deal with issues, we must recognize there are often root causes. The surface problem is only the visible part of the iceberg. When we only address what we can see and leave the underlying issues unattended, the cycle continues. It is akin to cutting branches and leaving the root. When we find ourselves reacting in ways that surprise us, it might be a sign of some underlying trauma, and perhaps, we have never stopped to process the pains from that experience. The first step to

RECOGNIZE YOUR FEARS AND THEIR DEEP-SEATED CAUSES.

healing is to recognize our fears and their deep-seated causes. After this, we must pay attention to how they inhibit us from having healthy expectations and experiences in our relationships, especially potential marriage relationships.

When Jesus healed, we often see that he sorted through all the layers of age-long and lifelong issues. He first took care of the spirit and soul, so that when the physical healing followed, it could be sustained.

I noticed this when I was pondering on the story of the man at the pool of Bethesda. We all know the story. Jesus asked if he wanted to be healed. The man went off in a totally different tangent in his response: "I have no one to help me get in the pool."

I used to think he was just full of unbelief and could not recognize this time of visitation. But before you pass this same judgement, pause a moment and think of this. Have you ever been at a place where you passed through your darkest moments, and you were all alone? The accusations you faced, the job or relationship you lost, or the sickness that racked your body was bad enough. But the feeling of abandonment and betrayal by those who you thought you could count on weighed heavy enough to crush your soul. Maybe it was from that place of emotional pain that the man's seemingly unbelieving response came. Otherwise, he really could just have asked Jesus to help him get into the pool.

You see, his biggest pain was not his crippled legs. It was that he had *no one*! We were not created to be alone; the weight of aloneness can crush a human soul. He must have watched other sick folks by the pool who had families or friends to wait on them, to help them move around, and to keep them company. The wound in his heart must have deepened.

I don't think it was a coincidence that Jesus singled him out of the crowd. What happened that day was more than strengthening of limbs. A deep emotional gash was also healed. Jesus's action was a loud declaration: "You are not alone. You have me now. You don't need a relative, an angel, or the pool. I'm all that you need, and I am more than enough."

After seeing this, I noticed a trend for every healing and miracle Jesus did. He first spoke to the person, and healed their emotions, addressing the state of their soul and deeper issues that were not immediately obvious. For instance, he told Bartimaeus to come near, thus removing the shame and isolation he had lived with. For the woman with the issue of blood, he publicly restored her dignity and self-esteem. He was compassionate towards the parents who had just lost their daughter, identifying with their grief. With the paralyzed man, he addressed his sin before his paralysis. With the woman at the well, he helped her to see that her insatiable thirst for men was reflective of the longing in her soul for God.

NO SCAR IS TOO BIG OR SMALL FOR GOD TO HEAL.

Why did Jesus take this approach? While we pay great attention to physical health, wholeness in the soul and spirit is even more important. "The human spirit can endure a sick body, but who can bear a crushed spirit?" (Proverbs 18:14). When we have wounds in our soul or spirit such as lack of trust, fear of being alone, fear of being vulnerable, or fear of mistreatment in marriage, God is eager to address them and bring us full healing.

At the end of this chapter, we will have a chance to reflect more deeply on our experiences, beliefs, and possible wounds that God may want to heal in us or truths he may want us to believe. In some cases, we will find that while we believe God's Word concerning a particular area of our lives, the picture implanted in our subconscious mind is in exact contrast, and so our actions and choices don't seem to align with our professed beliefs. You will have the opportunity to resist the Devil's lies and "fix your thoughts on what is true, and honourable, and right, and pure, and lovely, and admirable" (Philippians 4:8).

In some cases, we may consider finding someone with a godly perspective to provide some guidance in sorting out the negative emotions associated with these experiences. In my practice as a Christian counsellor, I have seen God sift through layers of these wounds to bring healing to clients, so I recommend getting professional counselling where necessary. As you pause and carry out the exercise, I pray in Jesus's name that God uncovers these deep-seated wounds and causes the healing process to begin in us. Amen!

HEALED TO HEAL

When God heals us completely from our scars, we are able to use the same experiences to help others heal. Like Paul said in his letter to the Corinthians, God uses the worst of our pains and the darkest of our experiences to equip us for bringing healing to others.

> All praise to God, the Father of our Lord Jesus Christ. God is our merciful Father and the source of all comfort. He comforts us in all our troubles so that we can comfort others. When they are troubled, we will be able to give them the same comfort God has given us (2 Corinthians 1:3-4).

It is important that we receive this healing before we try to heal others. People who need to be healed sometimes end up being the physicians of other ailing people without realizing they are feeding the wounds of their clients or protégés in the process. A friend who is a nurse explained to me that the process for wound management was first to open up the hardened surface of the wound; only then will the medication be applied. This is because the hardened surface is often a sign of false healing, and if treated on the surface only, the wound could become infected and fester.

For example, I met a lady who supported women in abusive relationships and marriages. The work she did with women in this situation was impressive and her passion was unmistakable. However, it wasn't long before I noticed her strong, negative reactions to men. I soon realized that she was once in an abusive relationship in which she was voiceless. I can't help thinking of her attitude towards men as retaliating for the abuse meted out to her by her ex.

> **WHEN GOD HEALS US, WE CAN HELP OTHERS HEAL.**

I'm a firm proponent of women not subjecting themselves to abuse or toxic relationships. However, we need to watch out for the blurry line that separates good judgement and being liberated from the other extreme of painting all men with the same brush because of our experience with less than noble men.

We have to be careful not to build our personalities, advocacy, and platforms from a place of hurt that we have not fully recovered from, especially for those of us called to bring healing to others. Otherwise, we will inflict our hurts on them. We have to allow God to purify the streams of our hearts, so that we can bring true release and refreshment, rather than ooze bitter waters. We have to first do the hard work of removing the log from our eyes, so we'll have the clarity to help others remove the speck in theirs. If we do not, while there may be outward results, we will also be doing damage by projecting our bitterness, anger, fear, and paranoia on others. As vessels that God wants to use to heal and minister to others, we must constantly reappraise our own hurts and bring them the cross of Jesus Christ to receive his healing balm. Otherwise, we will keep covering wounds with Band-Aids until they fester.

Of course, healing doesn't mean the incident didn't take place. We may still remember the harm done, but we can live without the effects dictating the course of our lives. One of the signs that you are truly healed is that the memory of the wound no longer brings pain. Eventually, we may even find that we are better off than we would have been if the incident hadn't taken place.

For instance, Joseph had painful experiences: being rejected by his brothers, sold into slavery, and falsely accused. But God restored him. His full healing was obvious in his statement to his brothers: God meant it for good. As a result, he was able to forgive his brothers with open arms.

THE PAIN THAT BROKE US HAS POTENTIAL TO BUILD US.

Often, our experience as a whole was traumatic – like Joseph's. It's OK to mourn whatever loss we've experienced. But at a closer glance, we might also find some bits and pieces that weren't entirely bad. Even the worst of experiences or relationships may have drawn us closer to God, made us wiser, taught us a lesson, or helped develop some positive character traits. Identifying these positives can mentally make it easier to forgive and heal from the damages from the experiences. Romans 5:3-5 says:

> We can rejoice, too, when we run into problems and trials, for we know that they help us develop endurance. And endurance develops strength of character, and character strengthens our confident hope of salvation. And this hope will not lead to disappointment. For we know how dearly God loves us, because he has given us the Holy Spirit to fill our hearts with his love.

The pain that broke us has the potential to build in us more strength and resilience than we imagine.

God is a redeemer. Once we are able to let go and release our experiences to him, we will find that in his hands, they become building blocks for what he wants to do with our lives. As Romans 8:28 says, "And we know that God causes everything to work together for the good of those who love God and are called according to his purpose for them."

A NEW BEGINNING

At one point, my tablet had been misbehaving, going on and off at will and freezing for long intervals. I'd sent it for repairs and was told it had battery issues. The cost for replacement was ridiculous, so I decided I'd let it be. One morning I restarted it and rushed out the door for a training programme.

To my utmost surprise, I came back home in the evening to a brand new tab. All the long-standing issues had been resolved. I realized that in my hurry, instead of the "restart" button, I had pressed the "reset" button, and so the factory settings had been restored! It turned out the battery wasn't the problem after all. I had overloaded the disc space with too much data.

While praying the next morning, I heard myself saying, "Lord, wipe the slate of my life clean so you can begin again with me." It felt symbolic to me, that God was pressing the "reset" button and bringing me into a new beginning.

One thing I am certain God wants to do with you is to bring healing, wholeness, and a new beginning into your life. He has done this over and over again throughout Scripture. When Israel had forsaken his covenant and was taken into exile, God gave them hope that he was doing something new:

> But forget all that –
>   it is nothing compared to what I am going to do.
> For I am about to do something new.
>   See, I have already begun! Do you not see it?
> I will make a pathway through the wilderness.
>   I will create rivers in the dry wasteland
>   (Isaiah 43:18-19).

The new thing God was doing included a promise to send a servant who would restore his people, a promise we hear in Isaiah 61 and fulfilled in Jesus. I love Isaiah 61; it's an anchor Scripture for me. It describes how the servant heals the broken-hearted, comforts those who mourn, and sets captives free. In verse three, we see their pain is transformed into praise:

> To all who mourn in Israel,
>> he will give a crown of beauty for ashes,
> a joyous blessing instead of mourning,
>> festive praise instead of despair.

Complete healing and restoration are connected to worship. They often come when we worship even if we are still in pain. Job's situation changed when he turned his focus from his suffering to God's awesomeness. For the first time, he was able to see from God's perspective. As a result, he was able to forgive his friends and intercede for them. In the same vein, after the ten lepers were healed, the one who came back to thank Jesus was told, "Your faith has healed you" (Luke 17:19). His worship was the completion of his healing. Isaiah 61:4 goes on to say:

> They will rebuild the ancient ruins,
>> repairing cities destroyed long ago.
> They will revive them,
>> though they have been deserted for many
>> generations.

When God's healed people come into their fullness and wholeness, they in turn build, restore society, and fully function in the assignment God has for them.

I have seen how God can heal even the worst scars in amazing ways, turning them into a beautiful ministry. A dear friend narrated how she was repeatedly raped by people she respected and trusted when she was only 19. For a long time, she felt unworthy, believing the lie that God could not use her because she was no longer a virgin. She blamed herself.

God helped her to overcome these feelings. Her hurt showed her how much she needed God. Today, she says that not only has she forgiven the perpetrators, she is able to relate with them without any ill-feeling. Her full healing came when she was able to release herself of blame.

As an undergraduate she started a ministry through which she has ministered to other people who have experienced rape, rejection, neglect from family, broken relationships, or low self-esteem. God has always given her the right word for each person which helped to bring about the healing they needed. She is also a music minister and worship leader. You can't miss her vulnerability with God when she leads a worship session. Her experience has made it easy for her to totally surrender with reckless abandon to God.

HEALING AND RESTORATION ARE CONNECTED TO WORSHIP.

My friend's story reminds us that there are no scars too big or too small for God to heal. He wants to make us whole. He redeems, restores, rebuilds. He is doing a new thing. So, let's trade in our ashes for a crown of beauty.

Happily Ever After Starts Here

Reflections

- What experiences in your life have left you scarred?

  _____
  _____
  _____
  _____

- What harmful beliefs or mindsets have you learned from others?

  _____
  _____
  _____
  _____

- How have these experiences and mindsets affected your perspective of yourself, your beliefs about God, and your expectations of relationships?

  _____
  _____
  _____
  _____

- Take time to read through the scars mentioned in the chapter again. Do any of them resonate with you?

  _____
  _____
  _____
  _____
  _____
  _____

Exercise

- Spend some time creating notes about the experiences and beliefs you identified that may have affected you negatively. What was painful about these experiences? Where does it still hurt?

_____

_____

_____

_____

_____

_____

_____

- Picture Jesus on the cross, suffering and wounded. Reflect on this image of Jesus, who knows what it is like to suffer as a human. Pause to pray and ask God what he would say to you about these experiences. Ask him to reveal his truth, love, and healing to you.

- Consider if you would need to get professional counselling. It might be helpful to find someone with a godly perspective to provide some guidance and hand holding in sorting out negative emotions associated with these experiences.

What the Bible says about healing and restoration

"I will give you back your health
   and heal your wounds," says the Lord.
"For you are called an outcast –
   'Jerusalem for whom no one cares'"
      (Jeremiah 30:17).

7

Sexual Purity
– A Myth?

We were watching a movie in a friend's living room on a Saturday afternoon. We got to that scene where it goes all romantic with sizzling sex. I started to feel uneasy, but looking around the room, everyone else seemed cool.

Oh, dear, something must be wrong with me. How come I'm the only one unable to sit through a sex scene and be cool?

I motioned at the TV set. "Hey girls, am I the only one who's feeling something here?"

"Of course not, we are all feeling it too," they admitted reluctantly.

"Oh, thank goodness! So how are you coping?" I was hoping to get a tip or two on how to survive my own ordeal, or at least be able to watch sexual scenes with such brazen steel.

They shrugged and the conversation ended.

We live in a world with more sexual images and conversations put in front of us than ever before. Sensuality lurks like landmines, showing up in almost every movie, song, advert, book, and seemingly harmless conversation. Our quest for purity is being encroached upon daily.

But sex is a surprisingly hushed subject in our churches. I'm honestly curious about sex, and my questions have made people uncomfortable. I've been told to keep quiet, that I am carnally minded, crazy, or even not born again.

So, I understand why Christian singles might not talk about it freely lest they be labelled immoral, whether they are sexually active or not. But then again, even married people in my circles rarely discuss sex.

We need to understand that talk about sex is not sinful in and of itself. Sexual thoughts and urges are things the average person faces each and every day. It is part of being human. Never mind our pious looks and sanctified vocabulary when we come to church. Much as we hate to admit it, we want sex, and we want it really bad!

There's nothing wrong with desire. Sex is a pleasurable experience, the climax of physical intimacy that can happen between two humans. It is a gift from God to his children to be enjoyed in marriage – and I look forward to enjoying sex as sanctioned by God.

But the forbidden often holds the strongest appeal, especially when hormones are raging. Singles who are determined to keep God's command on sexual purity are in a battlefield.

Still, I'm convinced that through the help of the Holy Spirit and discipline, sexual purity is possible. And it is worth it! Saving sex for marriage builds a foundation for healthy, clear-minded dating and trusting, guilt-free intimacy and pleasure in marriage. In the meantime, it gives us peace of mind instead of fearing consequences such as unwanted pregnancy, sexually transmitted diseases, and the shame of being discovered. Obeying God gives us confidence to approach him and develops virtues in us, such as patience, sacrifice, and self-control.

WHAT THE WORLD SAYS ABOUT SEX

There are a lot of speculation and myths around sex which, if embraced even unwittingly, would have us sidetracked and misguided. A lot of the things we've been told about sex are lies intended to undermine our conviction to pursue sexual purity. Let's set the record straight and tackle these myths before we go on to the truth of God's Word and his design for sex.

"Everyone's doing it"

Sometime ago, I was having a conversation with a friend and the discussion veered off to mature single ladies and how they cope with sexual pressure. He believed that 90 per cent of single, born-again, tongue-speaking Christian ladies waiting for Prince Charming have a "back-up plan" – a partner somewhere, married or single, who funds their lifestyle in exchange for booty-calls. I doubted his estimate because I am surrounded by mature single ladies. Though I can't vouch for everyone, the statistics would be the inverse, in my opinion. I couldn't help thinking, *Who are these people in his circle?*

When you hear blanket and generalizing statements like "all men cheat", "all women are sleeping around", and of course "everyone is doing it", it's often someone making an assumption based on their frame of reference. If you find these negative statements describe the company you keep, think twice about who you are surrounding yourself with.

"Every man wants to sleep with you"

I was shocked when a friend whom I had started to see as a brother began telling me how he wanted to sleep with me. His excuse? "Don't be so naïve. The only men who don't want to sleep with you are your father and your brother."

In another incident, I was trying to counsel a junior colleague who had been having problems in his relationship. He moved on and started a relationship with another lady – in just a couple of weeks. According to him, "Ladies are like dogs because

WE NEED TO BE CAREFUL WHO WE LISTEN TO.

anyone could own them potentially, so the earlier you made your move, the better for you." My jaw hit the floor. I couldn't even find any response for him.

However, I know there are still many honourable men who won't take advantage of you, even when you are in a vulnerable position. I have a much older married friend who used to dote on me, call me all the time, and come to check on me at work. At some point, I became uncomfortable and started to avoid him, wondering if there was more to the attention he was giving me. One day I ran into him and his wife. He said, "I know you've been avoiding me." I felt embarrassed. Over the years, he has proven to be like a father to me. I have since concluded that not every man wants to sleep with you.

Premising all relationships between men and women on sex is perversion and a complete departure from how God intended. This erroneous notion makes a lot of ladies expect that they have to give sex in exchange for favours. In 1 Timothy 5:2, Paul described how the relationship between men and women should be: "Treat older women as you would your mother, and treat younger women with all purity as you would your own sisters."

We need to be careful who we listen to, otherwise, we'll open ourselves to lies which leave us more susceptible to sin.

"You need to know if you're sexually compatible with your future spouse"

Some people argue that since you'll be having sex with just one person for the rest of your life, then you want to be sure it's going to be good. Others say that to make the wedding night perfect and eliminate all the clumsiness that comes with first-time sex, you need to get enough practice ahead of the big day. Some say sex is necessary for intimacy and bonding if you are really serious with each other. Others insist that no man will marry you without sex. Unfortunately, a lot of men have used this as a bait to demand sex saying, "After all, we'll be getting married." Lots of ladies fall for this.

Sexual compatibility, like every other aspect of marriage, is a skill spouses can work on together through patience, communication, and understanding. My female friends who got married as virgins have shared their honeymoon experiences with me. The first few days or weeks were quite bumpy, but it got better and better from there on. They say it's exciting to learn the ropes and finally get to enjoy sex with the one person they've committed to spend the rest of their lives with. That is, in fact, when the bonding takes place.

It seems to me that those who go experimenting because they want a "perfect" wedding night are not patient enough nor willing to put in the work required to build a satisfying sexual relationship. Instead, they might end up going from one sexual partner to another. How do you even measure the level of sexual compatibility that makes you decide this is the right one?

"Better to have kids first; marriage can come later"

An influential woman in Nigeria recently got pregnant out of wedlock. People were shocked, because she was a big advocate of sexual purity and a role model for many of her young followers. She offered an apology and explanation saying she had taken that path because she didn't want to have children in her 40s or have fertility issues later in life.

Of course, it is easier to have children at a younger age. Fears of your eggs drying up, early menopause, and slimmer chances of having children have driven women to have pre-marital sex. Some families even have strong traditions that mandate any intending bride to get pregnant before the wedding to forestall incidences of infertility in the future of the marriage.

It is true that as a woman gets older, her fertility starts to decline. However, research and medical technology have proven that older women do not necessarily have to be infertile. In a later chapter, I'll talk about how single women of faith can navigate their desires for children in ways that trust and honour God.

WHAT DOES GOD'S WORD SAY ABOUT SEX?

We live in an age of permissiveness where people are encouraged to go after whatever makes them happy. Gradually our frame of reference has shifted from the Word of God to our own personal "truths."

People could easily say it would make them happy to have what someone else has, sleep with a certain person, or get revenge. Would their happiness justify them committing theft, adultery, or murder? Imagine what the world would be like if we all went after instant gratification just to be happy. In Thomas Hobbes' words, life would be "nasty, brutish, and short".

If we deliberately deviate from the Word of God, we should expect consequences. According to God, sex is reserved for marriage, and sex outside marriage brings judgement: "Give honour to marriage, and remain faithful to one another in marriage. God will surely judge people who are immoral and those who commit adultery" (Hebrews 13:4).

WHEN YOU'RE TEMPTED, IT'S NOT TIME TO NEGOTIATE.

I've heard people say, "Well, sin is sin. Lying is as much sin as having sex outside marriage, so don't judge others unless you've never told a lie yourself." Not to discount one sin or glorify another, nor to say, "my sin is better than yours", but I find it interesting that in lists of sins, sexual sins come first in all of these Scriptures (emphasis mine):

> Let there be no *sexual immorality, impurity*, or greed among you. Such sins have no place among God's people (Ephesians 5:3).

When you follow the desires of your sinful nature, the results are very clear: *sexual immorality, impurity, lustful pleasures*, idolatry, sorcery, hostility, quarrelling, jealousy, outbursts of anger, selfish ambition, dissension, division (Galatians 5:19-20).

Being filled with all unrighteousness, *sexual immorality*, wickedness, covetousness, maliciousness; full of envy, murder, strife, deceit, evil-mindedness (Romans 1:29 NKJV, emphasis mine).

I don't think this is just a coincidence. I think sexual sin is singled out because there is a way that sexual sin is different from every other sin: sex affects your own body. Our culture, like the culture in Corinth, sometimes deceives us that what we do in our bodies has no spiritual significance. But sex causes deep unity between people who engage in it. The Holy Spirit also lives in our bodies and our bodies are parts of Christ. That's what Paul pointed out in response to the Corinthians:

Don't you realize that your bodies are actually parts of Christ? Should a man take his body, which is part of Christ, and join it to a prostitute? Never! And don't you realize that if a man joins himself to a prostitute, he becomes one body with her? For the Scriptures say, "The two are united into one." But the person who is joined to the Lord is one spirit with him.

Run from sexual sin! No other sin so clearly affects the body as this one does. For sexual immorality is a sin against your own body. Don't you realize that your body is the temple of the Holy Spirit, who lives in you and was given to you by God? You do not belong to yourself, for God bought you with a high price. So you must honour God with your body (1 Corinthians 6:15-20).

The high stakes explain why the Bible is very clear what to do when faced with sexual temptation – it says to *flee* (1 Corinthians 6:18; 2 Timothy 2:22 KJV). It's not time to negotiate. It's not time to talk about it. There's just one thing to do . . . run! And, for the record, *flee* means "to run away from a place or situation of danger". So, when sexual temptation comes knocking, know for sure that danger lurks just around the corner. Run for dear life. If you have to leave your coat behind like Joseph, just do it!

This isn't a Pharisee's rulebook seeking to make your single life a misery. Rather, it is about setting healthy and safe boundaries for your physical, emotional, and spiritual well-being. Sin wants control of your body, soul, and spirit. We can't exercise self-control on our own. We need to give ourselves fully to God.

If you are pursuing sexual purity and still struggle, I understand that. Don't give up, saying you can't help it. Depend on the help of the Holy Spirit: "But if through the power of the Spirit you put to death the deeds of your sinful nature, you will live" (Romans 8:13).

If, like me, you're serious about not stepping out of God's boundaries where sex is concerned, here's how you can flee from temptation and honour God with your body.

STAYING SEXUALLY PURE

See no evil, hear no evil, speak no evil

Christians often quote the biblical proverb "Guard your heart above all else" to encourage people to avoid emotional entanglement; but in biblical times, people believed the intellect, emotions, and will came from the heart (Proverbs 4:23).[3] So we could translate this proverb for modern readers as "guard your mind above all else". Psychologists

3   John H. Walton, *The Lost World of Genesis 1: Ancient Cosmology and the Origins Debate,* (Downers Grove, IL: IVP, 2009), 18.

SEXUAL SIN AFFECTS YOUR OWN BODY.

have concluded that the mind is the greatest sex organ. We need to pay attention to the kind of thoughts we allow into it. They are sown as seeds, but soon blossom into full-grown trees. The mind is the gateway to our lives. As the gatekeepers, we have to take charge of what we allow through.

I was catching up with an old friend on the phone. I was enjoying the intelligent conversation when it began to turn sexual. Somewhat curious, and against my better judgement, I tried to follow along. Suddenly I felt like something inside my soul was being stripped and exploited. Thankfully, I was able to shut down the conversation before more harm was done, and I stopped taking his calls.

Another time, I had colleagues who would send emails with adult content and cartoons. These things start off seemingly harmless, so you accommodate them easily. Soon you start to feel comfortable with them, and then they become addictive. Then one day they sent a five-minute pornographic video. As I watched it, I suddenly felt like something was trying to forcefully get into my soulish realm. It was a big tussle. I was gagging as I spent the next 10 minutes praying in the Holy Spirit, fighting to resist it. This may sound like fiction but it wasn't. Thankfully, I overcame that episode, and once it was over, I called the parties involved, warning them never again to send me such things.

"Oh, you want to tell me you didn't enjoy watching it?" one of them teased. I saw how this was a battle for my soul, so I promised to forward any such emails to Human Resources if they ever sent them my way again. That was the last they sent to me.

Do you realize how much damage pornography is causing in our world today? Studies have linked porn to infidelity, shown that it makes real-life sex less enjoyable, and shown that pornography has the same effect on the brains of sex

THE MIND IS THE GATEWAY TO OUR LIVES.

addicts that drugs have on drug addicts.[4] Pornography addictions destroy individuals, their present and future relationships, and often lead to disturbing or even violent re-enactments.

These battles are not carnal. If the Devil cannot get you, then he may send people around you to gain access to you. You can't afford to be nice about matters like these. Sometimes you have to be ready to lose friends or risk being uncool, just so you don't lose the sanctity of your soul.

It's not only the extreme of pornography that we need to guard ourselves against. As the Christian Booksellers Association used to say, "What goes into a mind comes out in a life." For instance, there's a reason why TV programmes are called *programmes* – they are designed to shape our perspective, programming us into a certain kind of person. So, we need to watch what we watch. We need to be mindful of what we read, what we listen to, the conversations we have, the company we keep, and the places we visit both online and offline.

Some people may argue, "I'm not under 17, and after all, isn't sex just meant to be a normal biological thing that happens between adults?" But having been exposed as a child to sexually explicit content by reading my cousin's adult magazines, I realized how powerful my mind is in capturing information and playing it back, even up to several years later. Just by being around me, you can tell what I've been watching or listening to – whether good or bad. Knowing this, I have gradually learned what the triggers are for me and worked hard to sift the information I take in.

---

4   Guy Kelly, "The scary effects of pornography: how the 21st century's acute addiction is rewiring our brains," *Telegraph*. 11 September 2017. https://www.telegraph.co.uk/men/thinking-man/scary-effects-pornography-21st-centurys-accute-addiction-rewiring/.

While they may seem harmless, I have deliberately withdrawn from reading some genres of novels and particular authors. The same goes for music that affects my mood negatively. I've had to leave very popular social media groups and unfollow lots of people I like because the ideologies they promote are discordant to the values I'm working hard to uphold. Before I decide to watch a film, I ask if there are sex scenes. Some people may think of these as extreme measures, but a Yoruba proverb translates to say, "If the eyes will not see evil, the whole body must be the antidote", meaning that we must run away from evil we don't want our eyes to see. Another says, "If we do not wish for our eyes to be poked by a long stick, we must learn to look at it from a distance."

The information we take in shapes our thinking and gradually dictates the course of our lives. As Christian single ladies in an over-sexualized society, we must make a deliberate effort to fill our minds, hearts, and souls with only what is pleasing to God. Philippians 4:8 holds up a high standard: "Now, dear brothers and sisters, one final thing. Fix your thoughts on what is true, and honorable, and right, and pure, and lovely, and admirable. Think about things that are excellent and worthy of praise." As we fill our hearts with good things, we will find we overflow with goodness and godliness.

Accept protection and correction

I often needed to travel for work. My travel companions would watch over me like hawks keeping predators away. Several times, my male colleagues interrogated me when I had a conversation with a male they were not familiar with. I'd roll my eyes and say, "Are you my father?" I didn't think I owed them an explanation.

But they had their reasons. As an adventurer, I loved discovering new places when I travelled for work. I had made foolish mistakes, like hopping into a van with a total stranger who wanted to "show me the town" in the thick of the night, driving miles to the middle of nowhere in a country I wasn't familiar with. Now I can't help thinking with dread, what if something had happened to me? No one would have known where I was, and I would have been beyond rescue. If God had not helped me, I could have been in big trouble.

So, although I did not like it at the time, in retrospect I am grateful for how God has used people around me to hold me accountable unrelentingly. If not for the timely wisdom of others – which, thankfully, I usually embraced – I could have fallen into ditches that I didn't see coming.

Other people can also alert you to outside threats you may not be aware of. Once a colleague from another section of the company came around to our office and began talking about me with my friends. I ignored them. Apparently, he observed to my friends how a senior colleague doted on me and said I must be dating the man. My friends not only corrected that impression, but also vouched that I was not the kind of lady to date a married man. The colleague from the other office wasn't convinced. Thinking he would get extra bragging rights if he could snatch someone so "hard-to-get", he placed a bet to get me by all means conceivable. Then moments after he left, my friends broke the "guy code" by telling me, "Bookie, watch out for that guy; he's out to get you."

Another reality as women is that we are designed so differently from men that we may underestimate or misjudge men's minds and intentions. We may consider ourselves very savvy and perceptive when it comes to reading other women, but at certain times it takes another man to see through another man and foresee a potentially dangerous situation.

As a single, full-grown woman in your own right, you very likely pay your own bills and make your own decisions without having to revert to anyone. It's both commendable and necessary for survival. However, much as we must embrace being independent, we cannot outgrow having other people look out for us. It's both foolhardy and proud to think we're never going to need input from others to get on well with our lives. Like the Bible says, "People who despise advice are asking for trouble" (Proverbs 13:13) and "There is safety in having many advisers" (Proverbs 11:14).

Set boundaries and don't be afraid to say no

Once, a guy had asked to take me out on a date. He enquired if I had a curfew.

"Yes, 9 p.m.," I replied matter-of-factly.

He was taken aback. "So, what would happen if you don't get home at 9 p.m.; your dad's going to be mad or something?"

I laughed. "No, I'm a 30-something-year-old woman, and my dad has no idea where I am at any time of the day. It's just my rules."

Another fellow invited me to hang out after work. I had thought we'd go and see a movie or something, but I finally gave up when I didn't hear from him that evening. Then my phone rang at about 9 p.m. He wanted to know if I was still up for the night out.

"At this time?" What I meant was, *Are you crazy?*

"Oh, the fun is just starting now. We can hang out a bit, then go club-hopping until around 1 a.m., then we head back."

"No, thanks!" I didn't have to think about it twice. Why put yourself in a precarious situation? Don't they say sins happen under the cover of darkness?

More times than not, we unwittingly walk into traps because we do not take proactive steps to forestall them.

As a single lady, you must develop the discipline of setting healthy boundaries. Examples of such boundaries would be setting a curfew when out on a date. As much as possible, minimize hosting male visitors, especially if you live alone. You can always meet at public places. Define what "boyfriend time" is. Don't let other men – whether a married colleague, friend, or pastor – call you or spend time with you during those late hours. Boundaries could also mean sharing your plans with someone with whom you can be totally honest. She can hold you accountable, help you review your activities, and point out potential pitfalls to you.

Setting boundaries also means avoiding undefined relationships. A friend once met the "man of her dreams". He was everything she had imagined in her partner, except they didn't share the same conviction. She wasn't sure if or when she'd ever find a man that ticked her boxes like he did . . . so she lingered. I let her know that was the easiest way to fall into sexual sin. Since you can't even tell if you're dating or what exactly you are doing, how then do you negotiate the terms or lay down ground rules? It's only a matter of time until you start having sex.

DEFINE WHAT "BOYFRIEND TIME" IS.

When asked when to start having sex in a relationship, one non-Christian relationship expert said, "If you're in it for the long term, delay sex for as long as possible so that you can focus on the more important things like building communication, friendship, etc. However, if you don't see any future in it, then you might as well start having sex already." Even people who don't live by the rules of the Bible realize that undefined relationships make premarital sex more likely, and that premarital sex undermines long-term relationships. When you are in an undefined relationship, what you can't have can suddenly hold so much appeal. You're tempted to grab as much as you can out of it while it lasts. It makes you short-sighted and more vulnerable to compromise.

"Failing to plan is planning to fail," the saying goes. Foresight and shrewdness are essential tools in our survival kit as single ladies. We have to take them along everywhere we go. So set your boundaries ahead of time, and never be afraid to turn down a request you're not comfortable with. Now, I'm not saying every guy will try to have his way with you, but why put yourself in a precarious situation in the first place?

Often our gut feeling tells us when things are about to go wrong, but we are too afraid to say no, so we just go along with the scripted, harmful plan. Sometimes, we're responding to the constant admonishments we've heard from concerned folks who are eager to have us married off: "Oh, you have to be more flexible." "The guy has to see that you are willing to go the extra mile." or "You won't be taken seriously if you keep turning down dates." So we end up not wanting to offend anyone, ignoring the warning signs, and winding up in harm's way.

We have to realize that saying no to things that do not line up with our convictions is actually a sign of emotional maturity and stability. Quite a number of people lay in wait to prey on single ladies, and we need to be wise. People who want you to bend over backwards to please them are not looking out for your good. Anyone who really cares about you will not try to encroach on your boundaries, act like your concerns are paranoid, or try to guilt you into abandoning your principles. In fact, a good man will appreciate how your boundaries also protect his integrity, reputation, and relationship with his spouse or future spouse.

Understand your sexuality

Until very recently, talking about sex was a taboo in most African households. For some of us, our parents found it so difficult to have the "birds and bees" talk that perhaps all they said to us at puberty was, "Don't go near a boy. If a man touches you, you'll become pregnant." I learned of one girl who burst out crying believing she was pregnant because a boy in her class had tapped her! We have had to sort through some very confusing messages.

I remember a conversation that was a lifesaver for me. On our way back from a woman's programme in church, two single ladies mentioned feeling intense sexual craving after their monthly cycles. I'm shy to say that at 29, I was hearing it for the first time. I read up on the topic and finally understood

123

that the woman's body is designed to feel more desire when we're ovulating as God's way of encouraging us to reproduce and enjoy it. I also realized why some days were worse than others and determined that if I could manage to survive those three to four days of raging hormones, then the rest of the time it would be easier for me to stay pure. What a deliverance!

Having sexual feelings as a single lady is not a sin. No, God created sex and it is a good thing. Sex is good, not dirty, despite some of our cultures' notions to the contrary. Sex is holy, not lewd, unlike what our present society depicts. We can affirm that God designed sex to be sacred and holy within the context of marriage. When you have sexual cravings, you have not sinned, it's just proof that your body functions are in good shape!

In a conversation with a friend, I told her about a guy who I was simply sexually attracted to, even though we really didn't have anything else in common. Of course, she laughed. "At this age, you ordinarily would be having regular sex, so it's just normal that your body wants it!" These days, when I'm thinking about sex and there's no one to talk to, I turn to God and say, "Oh well, I'm jolly looking forward to having sex; do make it happen soon." And I move on.

Sometimes instead of owning up to our sexual wants, we decide to play the ostrich, and that's why we get into trouble. If we don't acknowledge them, we can't deal with them. Pretending these feelings don't exist will not obliterate them.

Society sells us a lot of myths and lies about sex. Gain knowledge so you can turn the tides to your advantage. Understanding your sexuality in an academic manner will empower you to make the right choice ahead and stay in clear waters. Study God's perspective about sex from the Bible. Seek out inspiration from Joseph, who overcame temptation and was rewarded. Heed the warning of Samson, who experienced the consequences of his choices. Draw hope from David's repentance and restoration.

> **SEXUAL CRAVINGS JUST SHOW YOUR BODY FUNCTIONS ARE IN GOOD SHAPE!**

Remember, the Bible says temptation will come. You can't escape facing temptation. It is an ongoing battle: you deal with it each time, then wait for the next time. Even the Devil left Jesus "until the next opportunity came" (Luke 4:13).

That's why we must daily renew our minds; it's not a one-off exercise. Even in marriage, you will still battle sexual attraction to people who are not your spouse . . . or why do you think adultery exists?

Rather than be in denial, brace yourself to face it. Thankfully, it comes with waves and then a reprieve. What you do with the raging hormones while they last is what matters. Don't be shy about discussing your sexual feelings. However, be selective with whom you're discussing them and the environment to ensure you are

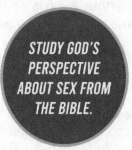

STUDY GOD'S PERSPECTIVE ABOUT SEX FROM THE BIBLE.

getting wise counsel and information rather than opening yourself up to perverse influences. Talk to God, confide in a trusted female, work through it, then move on from there.

Beware of thinking, "It can't happen to me"

Sometimes, we overestimate our own strength and thus overstep boundaries.

We may make unwise choices, thinking we can handle the temptation. Perhaps we stay out late with a guy, stay over at a male colleague's place to study or work, spend the night at a male friend's apartment, or entertain unnecessary visits from males when we live alone. Don't be foolish. Even if you are convinced you can handle it, you may not be able to speak for the other person.

Another dangerous situation is when you feel attracted to a wrong person, like a married person or non-believer, but you assume you are strong. Remember my friend who found her almost-dream man, except their Christian values did not align? If you feel attracted to someone you shouldn't date, don't tell that person. The same way the smell of blood draws sharks to their prey, when men of less-than-noble intentions find out you like them, they often pursue you as a conquest or prize. It is best to sort out your feelings outside of the already emotionally charged environment. Find someone to confide in who will help you through the process of coming out of the murky water. And no, your crush cannot be your accountability partner. He has no help to offer you. His intention could be the sin you should be fleeing from.

Sexual traps are not the exclusive reserve of lesser Christians. The greatest giants of faith such as David and Samson were as susceptible to sexual temptations as everyone else. That is why keeping a guard on your heart is a continual process. No wonder the Bible says to take heed if you think you stand, so that you don't fall.

You may be ready to throw your hands up and say, "What's the use? If they were tempted, how do I stand a chance?" But I believe that continuous discipline helps to build some muscles and habits. The things that used to easily trip you up become less and less appealing, and you're better prepared to make the right choices when it matters most.

Depend on God

Indeed, the weapons of our warfare are not carnal. Sometimes all we have is God's mercy to hold us up and help us even in times when we don't want to be helped.

When you are surrendered to God in your sexual life, the Devil will keep trying to trip you up and set you up in a big way, but God will set you up in a bigger way.

There was a time I was tired of being a good girl and determined that I would rebel drastically. While still trying to plan my sexual deviance, I tuned in, by divine providence, to a radio station. I caught a Christian single lady describing how she eventually gave in to her sexual craving. She had been in my exact situation and had successfully implemented her plan to go have a romp. She also shared her redemption story and her parting words were, "Don't do it. Keep holding on and trusting in God's plan for your life."

At that point, I could not doubt that God wanted to deliver me, and so I perished the thought. The pleasure of sexual adventure is so fleeting and short-lived that it is definitely not worth giving up for something so precious. Sexual purity is a choice that has made my life less complicated and painful, which is a better pay-off for me.

God is on hand to help us. Depend on him and commit to honour him. Even in times when we stray, he comes to our rescue. He is indeed our "very present help" (Psalm 46:1 KJV).

THE GOD OF GRACE

When we indulge in sexual sin, our relationship with God is the very first casualty. We are no longer able to approach God in all confidence. Even when we try to keep up appearances, we very likely will have to deal with guilt. If God is really all you've got, then you don't want to tamper with that relationship. Of course, illegitimate sex can also come with serious consequences, such as STIs, children without two parents to love and raise them, unhealthy soul ties, guilt, depression, or beclouded judgement that may end up in difficult marriages. It's best to avoid all this pain and suffering.

Even so, falling into sexual sin is not the end if we are willing to let God pick us up and help us start over on a fresh note with him. David committed adultery, lied, and even murdered the woman's husband to try to cover up his sin (sexual sin hardly happens without other accomplices, like hypocrisy). But finally, he brought his sin into the open and truly repented. You can read his confession of sin in Psalm 51. Although David still experienced severe and painful consequences – even to the treason and death of his son – God gave David another son, Solomon, whom God named Jedidiah because God greatly loved him (2 Samuel 12:25). God established Solomon on the throne, even though he was born out of a marriage that began on an adulterous note.

If you've sinned, first admit it to God. Genuinely repent from your heart and embrace God's forgiveness. Be sincerely willing to let go of the sinful lifestyle, even if you don't know how. As you surrender to God in this area and ask him to help you, you'll see him work out the details. Watch him begin the redemptive process in you.

Some people say that sexual purity is just for virgins. This is a ploy to make you give up before you even start. Virginity is not the same as sexual purity. The truth is, there are some virgins who indulge in everything short of full sexual intercourse; this is definitely not sexual purity. On the other hand, there are people who were once sexually active but now have made a commitment to abstain from sexual sin. If in the past you've been sexually involved, you can make a fresh start and make that choice for sexual purity and before God. You're no less than someone who's never had sex before.

If you haven't been sexually active, remember not to become proud in believing you're more worthy of God's love. While I was in church on a Sunday morning, an interesting conversation was going on in my mind during the sermon. I sensed a voice saying, "Do you know if you fell into sexual sin, I wouldn't love you any less than I do? You would remain precious and priceless to me."

> OUR RELATIONSHIP WITH GOD IS THE FIRST CASUALTY OF SEXUAL SIN.

Well, that was a bit of news to me. If I didn't know God's voice, I would have thought it was the Devil. "Yes, I know," I said, trying to sound like a sage, "But why are we even having this conversation?" It was as if the core of my holiness was being tampered with.

God went on to ask, "And why are you very uptight about this?"

"Well, Lord, I don't want to have this conversation. If it matters nothing to you that I commit fornication, then what about my testimony? Don't you know I have a reputation to protect?"

I felt like he smiled. I realized he was confronting my

motives and the intents of my heart. Was I only obeying to proudly defend my own honour or because I genuinely wanted to honour God?

We can't boast about our own righteousness or purity. Nothing we can do will make God love us any more or any less than he already does. God has saved us by his grace and will enable us to obey his commands with the help of the Holy Spirit. We might feel that we're obeying out of a sense of duty or trying to prove something, but what a reminder God whispered to me of his everlasting love and grace! *That* gives me a reason to obey – as a response of love and gratitude to him.

SEXUAL PURITY IS WORTH IT

Sexual temptation for a mature single lady is high. But so is the cost of giving in. Whatever gratification we enjoy from the temporary pleasure is not worth it. When we walk in purity, we exercise self-control, a fruit of the Spirit. Whether we're single or married, we'll always need to exercise self-discipline, whether it's avoiding sex before marriage or abstaining in a married season when sexual fulfilment may not be possible due to travel, illness, or another life circumstance. Staying pure has many benefits. If and when we do get married, our spouse will be able to trust us knowing that we have been able to resist temptation before. We can enjoy the bliss and blessings of marriage guilt-free.

We have a great destiny ahead and a specific role in the body of Christ. We can't afford to trade that off for moments of lusty pleasure, no matter how irresistible it may seem.

God is looking for lights in this dark and perverse world. I pray we would be vessels of honour, presenting our bodies, spirits, and souls to him in all holiness.

> And so, dear brothers and sisters, I plead with you to give your bodies to God because of all he has done for you. Let them be a living and holy sacrifice – the kind he will find acceptable. This is truly the way to

worship him. Don't copy the behaviour and customs of this world, but let God transform you into a new person by changing the way you think. Then you will learn to know God's will for you, which is good and pleasing and perfect (Romans 12:1-2).

The world's view of sex is in sharp contrast to God's. Sex amongst unmarried people is seen as fashionable, fun, and a biological response to natural instincts. However, God sees it as sin. As single ladies seeking to live sexually pure lives, God can give us the strength to diligently set a watch over our minds, the environments we visit, and the company we keep. This is the path to healthy relationships with God and other people, the path to peace of mind, holiness, and wholeness.

Happily Ever After Starts Here

Reflections

- What's your belief about sexual purity and abstinence? If you currently are not abstaining from sex, is abstinence something you would like to consider?

_____

_____

_____

_____

_____

- What are some boundaries you could set to protect your mind from sexual stimulation?

_____

_____

_____

_____

_____

- In which situations, times, environments, or company do you feel vulnerable to sexual temptation? What boundaries could help you avoid these situations?

_____

_____

_____

_____

_____

_____

_____

Exercise

- Take inventory of your media. Are there movies, music, books, images, feeds, subscriptions, accounts you follow, or other media that cause unhelpful sexual stimulation? Pray for the Holy Spirit's help and get rid of them.

- Contact a friend who has taken a stance for sexual purity. Find a time to discuss the questions above together. Ask your friend to check-in with you to keep you accountable to these boundaries.

What the Bible says about sexual purity

God's will is for you to be holy, so stay away from all sexual sin. Then each of you will control his own body and live in holiness and honour – not in lustful passion like the pagans who do not know God and his ways (1 Thessalonians 4:3-5).

Is There a Place for Single Ladies?

I remember when I was approached to write the "Diary of a Mature Single Lady" for a Facebook group of Christian women. I was both excited and curious. My task was to give the readers a peek into my daily experience in real time: the joys and struggles of being a single Christian lady in her 30s. I realized I would need to be real and share from a place of conviction. So I asked myself, "Is there a place for single ladies in the Bible?"

I must confess I wasn't expecting to find much. I didn't think women held much relevance in the Bible apart from being somebody's wife or mother, similar to our traditional societies. So how much less an unmarried lady? But no sooner did this thought cross my mind than names of biblical women leapt to mind in quick succession. There were plenty of single ladies who played very significant roles in their families and communities! This was a big eye-opener to the fact that the single lady actually has a place of relevance in God's plan and programming.

RUTH

Take Ruth for an example. It's almost an irony that she has become the poster child for perfect singlehood in Christendom today. Singles love to be referred to as "Ruths awaiting their

Boazes". True, we meet Ruth when she was single again after the loss of her husband. But the point of Ruth's story isn't really about her waiting around to get married.

When you start the book, it sounds like it is the story of Elimelech and Naomi. The opening pages had me wondering: why did Elimelech and his family leave Israel during the famine to go to Moab, an enemy nation? Could it be that he was out of God's will, and this was why he and his sons died? On and on my analysis went, then suddenly I stopped and asked, "Wait, what's the name of this book again, Ruth?"

How did a story which started in Israel, perhaps before Ruth was born, end up being named after her? Moreover, this book came as a disruption to the story of the judges. After many tales of Israel's judges with their anointing and their conquests, the historians paused to talk about a poor, alien, widow from a neighbouring enemy country. After her abrupt story, they continue to the next and final judge of Israel, Samuel. So how did Ruth even get into the story?

I believe that Ruth encountered the true God. She was convinced that aligning herself with the Jewish God as her own God and the Jewish people as her own people was the pathway to her destiny (Ruth 1:16). Even though her situation as a widow looked bleak and hopeless, she held on to her conviction. This made her follow a path which obviously was leading to a dead-end: no husband, no children, discrimination, and an abundance of poverty.

And guess what? She became the first female and the only non-Jew to have a book of the Bible named after her. She got married to Boaz, became the great-grandmother of David and a direct ancestor of Jesus. The story wasn't just about a poor, peasant widow; it was about God's purpose and the person who made herself available to birth it.

> RUTH'S STORY ISN'T REALLY ABOUT HER WAITING AROUND TO GET MARRIED.

What a sterling example of what God can do with anyone who decides to yield themselves completely to God and follow after his purposes, irrespective of their age, gender, marital status, race, nationality, and status in society.

A CLOUD OF WITNESSES

"Is there a place for single ladies?" Over and over, the Bible says: "YES!" I dug a little further into their stories and I found a common thread among these single ladies in the Bible.

The daughters of Zelophehad. A father was facing the misfortune of losing his family line, simply because he did not have a son to inherit from him. His daughters rose to the occasion. By insisting on getting their inheritance, they set a new precedent which became enshrined in the national constitution for generations to come (Numbers 27:1-11; 36:1-13).

Rahab. Her story opens with an account of her unsavoury lifestyle. She was a prostitute, albeit one with great discernment. She understood the things of the spirit; thus, she quickly aligned her ways with the living God and helped to save the Jewish spies. Through her, her entire household was saved from destruction and from her lineage came forth the Messiah (Joshua 2; 6:22-25). And did you know she was Ruth's other mother-in-law?

Esther. She survived a very rough childhood. Her parents were killed. She was taken captive to another country where her gracious uncle adopted her. He put her forward to participate in a beauty pageant when the king sought a bride. After a long and rigorous preparation, she became the queen of the country where she had once been a captive. Eventually, the time came for her to stand in the gap and put her life on the line for the salvation of an entire people. The purpose of her marriage to a heathen king was to save her people from the genocide plotted by an adversary.

Mary. She was a young and very ordinary lady, perhaps a peasant. She had to bear the shame and stigma of being pregnant as a single lady, which could even carry a death penalty in her culture. However, through her, the Saviour was born, and salvation came to the world.

Samaritan woman. She had been married five times but couldn't find fulfilment in any of her relationships. Soon she was back to where she started – being a single lady while still trying out a potential sixth husband. She was looking for love in all the wrong places. Her deepest needs and longings were unmet – until she found Jesus. Suddenly, she became the channel through which salvation flowed to her entire community (John 4:1-42).

Why had I never noticed these women were all single? When they were first introduced to us in the Bible and at the point of their God-encounters, they were never-married singles, engaged, widowed, divorced . . . but definitely unmarried. I find a common thread in all of these stories: these women, each of them single, were all a part of God's grand design to bring salvation to their families, communities, nation, and the world at large. We can see that the ladies profiled above didn't have it all together, but what mattered was that they had God's calling on their lives which they each fulfilled in various ways.

It could be, then, God's purpose for us as single ladies is to bring salvation and deliverance to our different spheres of influence. This is irrespective of your status or circumstances as a single lady – whether you are a single mother, divorced, widowed, advanced in age, or have a not-too-pretty and hurtful past. If you thought, "They're not talking about me here", think again. The Bible has shown over and over again that God can use unmarried women mightily for his purpose. It is therefore important to trust that God can and is using our waiting season for his greater purposes, which often seem hidden to ordinary eyes. We have to keep our eyes peeled on Jesus as the reason why we're doing what we're called to do. Otherwise, we'll soon lose focus and fall into dissension.

SERVE GOD IN THE ORDINARY

As these biblical women remind us, our everyday life can be our service to God. We serve God by serving people. Before God, both the clergy and the laity are equally called to serve him. God rewards us for serving faithfully, both in your local church and in your workplace or community, where you can represent him to people who may not know him. What counts is our faithfulness, no matter the place or position we're in. As Colossians 2:23-24 reminds us, "Work willingly at whatever you do, as though you were working for the Lord rather than for people. Remember that the Lord will give you an inheritance as your reward, and that the Master you are serving is Christ."

We don't need to do something spectacular to serve God. As God's stewards, the test we have to pass is the heart test. People may despise it, but God honours and rewards a meek and quiet spirit. It is not the same as a timid spirit; rather, it is power under control.

Sometimes we can become dissatisfied when the church limits the role of single women and does not allow us to serve in our area of ministry gifting. This can tempt us to dissension or rebellion. To avoid that, we should be OK with serving in whatever capacity we are allowed and see it as serving God who is the rewarder.

This is not in any way excusing the obstacles some church leaders might place in the ways of a woman in fulfilling her calling because she's single, but rather about obeying God in submitting to authority and trusting God to create room for us. By the Spirit of God, we are able to overcome obstacles with gentleness and God's wisdom at work in us.

When we are faithful in serving where we are, God will often promote us and reward us with greater responsibilities. I heard the story of a man whom God had called to be a prophet and had asked to serve in a particular ministry. However, the man was told that the only vacancy was for a janitor. He reluctantly took the role and started scrubbing toilets. The church authorities soon found that the toilet queues were

> WE DON'T NEED TO DO SOMETHING SPECTACULAR TO SERVE GOD.

getting longer; while waiting to use the toilet, people were getting words of prophecy from him! He was soon promoted to minister from the pulpit, where God had originally called him.

In the course of writing this book, I have met and interacted with single ladies who are serving the Lord in various fields, using their skills, talents, and abilities to serve their communities. I believe you'll be able to draw inspiration and motivation from some of them:

- Omotola works under precarious circumstances to help ladies in modern-day slavery get freedom through the *Rescue Africans in Slavery Organization.*

- Tomi is a critical care doctor. She cares for people in their darkest hours, ministering Christ through her deeds, as well as in words to those who are receptive.

- Rebecca uses social media platforms to teach financial literacy and help people build secure futures. Through her own experience, she also helps people at ground zero build or make career transitions.

- Mary has a mission to abandoned senior citizens: leading them to Christ, feeding them, and helping them live out the rest of their lives as comfortably as possible. She does this through the *Cavanaugh Lifecare Initiative.*

- Marian is a passionate trainer and financial consultant who uses her platform to simplify difficult concepts and help her students overcome their fears of numbers, so they can apply their financial skills in solving real-life problems.

- Hannah, my editor for this book, creates platforms for African authors so that their voices and unique messages will bless the body of Christ globally.

- Adetola is a policymaker and EdTech Advocate who uses her office to drive the infusion of STEM (Science Technology Engineering and Mathematics) and inclusion for women in STEM across Africa.

- Tosin, Coach Teedi, as she's fondly called by her pupils, is an early childhood educator who is running with her God-given vision to inculcate biblical wisdom and godly character in children at an early age, while raising them to become intelligent, creative, and innovative kids.

These are just a few examples of single ladies in our times who aren't waiting for marriage to start fulfilling their callings in God. As I already highlighted, you don't have to be doing something big to serve God. Some of us don't think much about it, but we are already doing these things. Still, we are touching lives and God notices.

DON'T WASTE YOUR WAIT

Can I be honest? Sometimes, I just want to get married, so I won't have to pursue my purpose anymore. I want to make marriage my escape. I dream I will find a man who's in pursuit of his own calling so I can hide under that. That would be just fine. It would be a lot easier than the discipline and the price I pay to become the full version of who God made me to be.

OUR PURPOSE IS BIGGER THAN FINDING A HUSBAND.

But I imagine for a moment that I got lucky. I met someone who fit this profile. I got onto the marriage train, only to find that he was as lost as I was. I would feel deceived, short-changed, and perhaps betrayed. There's no way I'd be happy in that marriage or relationship.

The source of frustration for many people, whether spouses or parents, is that we project our needs unto other people. We hope to live our dreams through them as they find their path. We'd be content with tagging along on the sidelines as their shadow. We want to make them our alibi for where we were when our purpose went missing. Maybe that will suffice for the foreseeable future. Often when we do not find our purpose from God, we hope to find it in other people, placing a heavy burden on them. When these unrealistic expectations are not met, it can damage the relationship.

But our purpose is bigger than just finding a husband and latching on to his purpose. In any case, we don't have husbands now. We can't wait for one to live on purpose. So what is the purpose God has for you and me, right where we are?

A guest speaker at a women's programme shared how she had attended a childhood friend's funeral. The friend had died in her early 40s. Reading through the deceased's biography, she became inconsolable. She couldn't seem to find any tangible achievements or signs that her friend had lived a fulfilled life. Rather, she had spent her last years consumed by bitterness over her husband's philandering. The preacher mourned not just for her friend's life that was cut short, but also for the potential that was never realized.

This taught her a very great lesson, giving her a new focus as a marriage counsellor in her church. She often had to counsel couples who were going through troubling times in their marriages and singles who had relationship issues or were anxious about marriage. She decided to take them through a session to find out what their passions and ministry giftings were.

They began to channel their energy into developing their passions, becoming positive people, and making positive contributions to their communities while they worked on resolving their relationship issues. Soon, they realized their spouses or partners were not the real issue after all. The pains were not wasted, but rather became an investment in other people, and in return, they found purpose and fulfilment.

The marriage counsellor worked with people to find their unique purposes, because God has designed us uniquely in line with the purpose we were created to fulfil. He put in us certain traits and strengths because of the work he has for us to do. The parable of the talents in Matthew reminds us that God has invested something in us that he wants us to use to serve him and our generation. It is folly to compare what he has given us with others or just leave it idle while waiting for an appropriate time. God expects us to invest what he has given us into other people, and he will hold us accountable.

If you're yet to discover what you can do or how you can affect others positively for God, I encourage you to take time to ask specifically for God to point you to those resources he already put in you and how best to use them to fulfil your purpose in him. Here are a few pointers that might help you identify what you're best equipped to do.

Skills, talents, abilities. Some things come naturally to us because they are our area of giftings, and we've been equipped by God to use them to affect our world positively for him. Some of us have been criticized by people around us or by society for traits that are actually strengths and we have come to see them as weaknesses. For example, people with oratory skills may have been shut down repeatedly as being talkative, especially in a society as ours where children should be seen but not heard.

In my case, I was discouraged from pursuing my love for the arts, because at the time, people in the arts were seen as the dregs of society. Even our head of school referred to arts students as "ramshackle". This discouraged me, so I tried to play safe by looking at other career options. But I'm grateful to God that today, through my writings and literary works, I am serving God and many people have been blessed.

> GOD EXPECTS US TO INVEST WHAT HE HAS GIVEN US INTO OTHER PEOPLE.

If this has been your situation, I would like to encourage that you go back to God. Ask him to unearth that skill or talent that you might have buried as a result of discouragement. He can empower you to develop and use your skills to bless the world.

Desire. God places certain desires in our hearts so we can pursue them relentlessly and easily find grace to fulfil them. Desire keeps us on track and in pursuit of the dream God has placed in our hearts. Even when time has passed, and the vicissitudes of life have buried those dreams that burned in our heart, our hearts never forget them and neither does God. Of course, not all our desires are necessarily from God and others may not be essential. But sometimes our desire represents an inner conviction from God.

When we let our desires go and surrender them to God, I have found they often become sanctified. Like seeds in the earth, they resurrect and return in a glorified state that only God can produce. For example, Moses knew in his heart that he was called to be a deliverer for the Israelites from Egypt. But he became an outlaw and vagabond. Under the circumstances, there was no hope that he could ever return to his people. Forty years later, God visited him to reawaken the dream. He became the greatest prophet and deliverer of the Old Testament and as symbol of the Messiah to come. In the same vein, God had shown Joseph visions of greatness and leadership, but he wound up as a slave, then a prisoner. There was no way those dreams could be fulfilled in the circumstances. But God turned that around, and Joseph became the most influential person of his day after Pharaoh.

As you read this, are there any desires that you firmly believe are in line with God's assignment for you, but you've given up on them? Perhaps by the natural look of things they seem impossible. I want you to pause now and take a minute to recommit them to God's hands in surrender. Leave them there and wait (no pun intended) to see how he will resurrect and multiply them beyond your imagination.

Life's experiences. Our experiences are often pointers to our assignment. To equip us for our purpose, God allows us to go down certain paths, which often become our greatest source of passion and compassion. They drive us to help other people who have to walk similar paths.

My friend Abiade had a hard time furthering her education after secondary school, as there was no one to sponsor her. Today she's not just a lawyer but also a youth advocate, using her time and resources to empower young people within her community with the education and skills they need to thrive and become useful contributors in the society. To date, her foundation has sponsored hundreds of youths. When I asked why she does what she does, her answer was: "There's no other way for me to live. I'd be as good as dead if I were not doing this."

THE TIME IS NOW

Often, our excuse for not living out our highest potential is simply that the conditions are not perfect. In fact, a lot of us are too afraid to step out of our comfort zones to move into what God has called us to. We have embraced an illusion of "the perfect time". We don't realize that the grace God offers freely to us will only be released when we have stepped into that place.

Psalm 90:12 says, "Teach us to realize the brevity of life, so that we may grow in wisdom." For a long time, I associated this verse of Scripture strictly with sermons preached at a funeral. Recently, I got another perspective on it. I saw the need to be accountable for our time and steward it wisely. We need to channel it into our life's purpose in a way that is rewarding to us and to God's kingdom, just like the faithful servants who invested their talents wisely. The greatest resource we've been given on earth is time. We can't afford to waste time idling, waiting for a man to arrive before we start to invest our talents and all the while missing our reward.

Life doesn't start after we get married. It also doesn't end on the earth. But the way we live on earth will determine how we live in eternity. Our reason for being on earth is not just to marry and have children. While these are important on the earth, in heaven we will be rewarded for our contribution to God's kingdom. We must not become blindsided to God's eternal purpose while on earth.

When the Corinthians were wondering whether they should get married, Paul advised them to focus on God's kingdom because the time was short:

WE HAVE EMBRACED AN ILLUSION OF "THE PERFECT TIME".

> But let me say this, dear brothers and sisters: The time that remains is very short. So from now on, those with wives should not focus only on their marriage. Those who weep or who rejoice or who buy things should not be absorbed by their weeping or their joy or their possessions. Those who use the things of the world should not become attached to them. For this world as we know it will soon pass away (1 Corinthians 7:29-31).

Paul also said that singleness affords us fewer distractions and responsibilities, so we can channel undivided attention towards the things of the Lord. In other words, God can use us for his purpose in unique ways because of our singleness.

This reminds me of what a guest minister said at a programme for singles. In earlier days, the singles used to be the envy of the church when it came to spiritual things. They were the ones who would show up at every prayer meeting, the ones who would volunteer at church outreaches, the ones who manifested the gifts of the Spirit. But it looks like we have now relegated spiritual things to the back burner in our quest to get married. A lot of ministers have taken advantage of this to pack their crusades full of programmes targeted at breaking the "yoke of singleness". We need to remember we are here for a purpose and pursue it! In fact, you may not be in this place forever. Don't waste your wait!

Jesus understood well that life is short, so we shouldn't put off our purpose. He knew he had only been apportioned 33 years on the earth, so he got to work. John 9:4 says, "We must quickly carry out the tasks assigned to us by the one who sent us. The night is coming, and then no one can work."

Some people said they wanted to follow Jesus, but they were looking for the perfect time to start. One first wanted to bury his father and another wanted to say goodbye to his family (Luke 9:57-62). But when Jesus sent out the disciples at the beginning of that chapter, his charge to them sounded something like, "Don't bother about having a picture-perfect wardrobe or a fat bank account before setting out on the assignment to preach the gospel. Eat whatever food you find and sleep wherever you find a spare bed."

In the entrepreneurial world, this is called "bootstrapping". You can also call it the "leap of faith". Sometimes, we have to go out on a limb. Our position may be unpopular and risky, but if our conviction is that it is of God, then it's a walk of faith we must all undertake.

We could continue on the path of least resistance and leave the outcomes and trajectory of our lives to gravity. Or we could make the hard decisions. Change comes at a price. It will require discipline and sacrifice, but it could decide the course of our lives for the next 20 to 40 years, if Jesus tarries. Like John Maxwell said, "Pay now, play later; play now, pay later. Either way, you pay."

LIFE DOESN'T START AFTER WE GET MARRIED.

God has a plan and a place for every person he created, including the unmarried lady irrespective of her age. In God's kingdom, there are no second- or third-class citizens. Don't buy into the lie that you are one and less deserving to be used by him. As biblical women remind us, God can use us in unlimited ways once we submit our agenda to him. So, refocus from seeking your own agenda to become kingdom-focused. Make it your ultimate goal to find God's purpose and run with it.

There's a purpose to every wait. What are you doing with yours?

Happily Ever After Starts Here

Reflections

- Have you ever felt you don't have much relevance in your community, church, family, or workplace because you are not married?

_____

_____

_____

_____

_____

_____

- Which single ladies inspire you with their purpose, whether biblical ones from this chapter, famous people, or people you know?

_____

_____

_____

_____

_____

- Can you think of any excuses you have made about why you aren't living out your purpose as a single lady? How would you respond to those excuses?

_____

_____

_____

_____

_____

Exercise

- Imagine you are making a curriculum vitae (CV) or résumé for life. List the skills, talents, and abilities you have. What desires has God given you? Add them to the document. What unique or formative life experiences have you had?

- Review your life résumé. What role do you think this résumé would fit? Don't think of it as a career, necessarily. Instead, ask what unique "job", purpose, or assignment God might have for you based on what he has already placed within you.

Skills, talents, and abilities:

_____

_____

Desires:

_____

_____

_____

Experiences:

_____

_____

_____

What the Bible says about single people

An unmarried man can spend his time doing the Lord's work and thinking how to please him . . . In the same way, a woman who is no longer married or has never been married can be devoted to the Lord and holy in body and in spirit (1 Corinthians 7:32, 34).

9

Money Matters

When an old schoolmate called me, the conversation gradually eased into the marriage terrain. Well, did I see that coming! It seems the only thing old friends want to talk about when reconnecting after several years. The onerous task, as usual, was to explain why I still wasn't married 20+ years after graduating from university. True to form, my friend started on the path of a tenable explanation for my "chronic singleness". Surely, there had to be one. It turned out to be one of the classic ones: "Maybe men find your success intimidating."

Wow, success according to whose definition? I wondered if I needed to publish my bank statement in the public domain to correct their mistaken assumptions about my fat bank account.

"I wish I had that kind of money that would really intimidate people!" I replied.

SHOULD A SINGLE LADY HAVE MONEY?

Now, to answer the question about if a lady who is unmarried should have money or not, I will start by asking another question: "Should a Christian have money?"

First of all, while we're on the earth, we're going to have to deal with money. Your marital status does not exempt you from basic needs. You cannot tender your singleness as an excuse to your landlord, at the grocery store, at the hospital, or even in school for free tuition. You still have the obligation to take care of your family members. Life's emergencies won't exempt you. So, all of us need to know how to use money as Christians. Jesus knew we would need to deal with money, so he spoke about it often.

> **HAVING MONEY IS NOT THE PROBLEM; LETTING IT HAVE YOU IS.**

Still, money is quite a controversial topic amongst Christians. Similar to how sex is seen as filthy, the mention of money in a sermon will make some people cringe and consider the pastor an apostate. For a long time, I struggled with understanding whether having money could reduce our ability to live holy lives and become an obstacle to getting into heaven.

Does the Bible say money is evil? What 1 Timothy 6:10 actually says is, "For the *love* of money is the root of all kinds of evil" (emphasis mine). Avarice makes people wander from the faith. Jesus says, "You cannot serve God and be enslaved to money" (Matthew 6:24). Note that this does not say that you cannot serve God if you have money. Rather, it says you cannot serve *both* God and money. Having money is not the problem; letting it have you is. Money often seeks to be the boss. We must determine upfront who the Boss is.

So money should be a servant, a tool in our hands. How we manage it is a test of our character. Our faithfulness in managing money qualifies us to be entrusted with true riches of the kingdom (Luke 16:1-13). One of the ways we prove faithful in managing money is by investing it into the lives of others. In Mark 10:21, Jesus told the young rich ruler that if he would invest his wealth into helping the poor, he would gain treasure in heaven. In contrast, the rich man who built barns to store his extra grain was called a fool by God because he focused only on investing in this life: "Yes, a person is a fool to store up earthly wealth but not have a rich relationship with God" (Luke 12:21; read 12:13-21).

These principles apply to all Christians, but I still haven't found any verse in the Bible that says a woman should not have money. For an example of biblical single women and money, I love the daughters of Zelophehad. In Numbers 27, these single ladies asked for their share of the land, which in those days was the measure of wealth. God approved them getting it. That also tells me that God is not opposed to single ladies having money or material possessions.

The Proverbs 31 woman in the Bible, who has been used as a benchmark of what a Christian woman should be, is a lady of no mean means. She was a woman of commerce who invested, traded, made profits, and owned properties. She worked hard and managed resources well. But did you know that Proverbs 31 is not just about married women? In fact, it was a poem from the king's mother admonishing her son about the type of wife he should seek to marry. He had to look for an unmarried woman who had the potential to become the "virtuous woman" of Proverbs 31. The truth is, if you are not virtuous as a single, marriage will not automatically confer virtue to you.

Whether we are male or female, I don't believe we have to apologize for being successful if we use the abilities and giftings God gives us, and God blesses us with financial and material resources. I also don't believe that single women should stop making conscious and significant progression in their careers because society sees that as intimidating.

If you are at a stage where you can afford to buy or own a house or property, go for it. If you don't feel comfortable living in your own house as a single lady (although I don't see why not), you may let it out and generate rental income from it. While society might have biases against single women having money, God does not.

All across Africa we can see how much blessing it brings to communities when women have money. Women reinvest up to 90 per cent of their income back into their families.[5] The

---

5   Maggie Germano, "How Women Can Change The World With Their Money Choices," *Forbes*, 22 September 2020, https://www.forbes.com/sites/maggiegermano/2020/09/22/how-women-can-change-the-world-with-their-money-choices/?sh=7e33db2c6138.

amazing strength of the African woman is the ability to create multiple streams of income to support her family. When a woman has a thriving business, her children are likely to be better educated and have better prospects for the future. My mum had up to three side businesses in addition to her full-time teaching job. That resilient spirit is still very present with us. In contemporary Nigerian society, for example, you can hardly find a woman who has not learned a trade – be it tailoring, catering, event planning, hairdressing, makeup artistry, photography, or at least a side business – irrespective of her level of education and profession.

I have said all of this to open our eyes to see how much value we bring to society and to the world. We women are very valuable and contributing members of any society. If we knew this, then we would be willing to invest in ourselves to attain our God-given potential – and we would become a blessing to our communities and the people around us.

> **HOW WE MANAGE MONEY IS A TEST OF OUR CHARACTER.**

WHAT'S YOUR MONEY MINDSET?

A mindset is a very powerful thing. It is a programming of the subconscious mind, which will dictate our perspective and approach to money. Let's talk about how we should think about money and the traps we often fall into.

Spend vs. earn and invest

Some of us don't have the right skills for earning money. Unfortunately, being unable to earn money has kept many women stuck in unhealthy relationships they should not be in because it's their meal ticket. We can also make poor choices because we need to **spend** money to give us our sense of self-worth.

Some ladies would go to any extent to get money. They may even give their bodies, God's precious and treasured temple, for money. They may live off of men who are not their husbands, with fancy names like *aristo*, *blessers*, and *sponsors*, or indulge in what they have now termed as *escort services* in exchange for money.

Wearing the latest fashions and living a lifestyle we can't afford is not bourgeois. In fact, the Bible calls it foolishness: "fools spend whatever they get" (Proverbs 21:20). While we may think we are living free from money worries, Horace once said, "He will always be a slave who does not know how to live upon a little."

God usually provides for our needs by giving us skills to enable us to **work and earn** money. Remember, God created us to work. Work existed in the Garden of Eden before the Fall. God worked to create the world. So, we all need to work for a living. We will talk more about how to do this in the next section.

God doesn't give us money just to spend, but rather to invest. I like to think of money as seed which is meant to be sown and multiplied. In the kingdom, we save to sow, to **invest** in kingdom purposes. Our seed grows into a tree. Trees provide food and shelter for God's creatures. That is the purpose of money when we invest it properly – it gives glory to God and blesses others.

Fear vs. trust

Sometimes our relationship with money is driven by fear. Life might have thrown its vicissitudes on you, and perhaps at some point, you struggled to pay your bills, missed payments, or had nothing left over when you managed to pay them. It would not be surprising if your relationship with money became one of fear, and you have become attuned to living in survival mode.

When our relationship with money is driven by fear or anxiety, we often make poor choices. For instance, we might stay in a toxic relationship or job, we might not be able to afford time for the things that matter to us, or we hold back from launching into our God-given assignments. Fear can drive us to either extreme: **amassing** like the rich fool (Luke 12:13-21) or **avoiding** like the man who buried his talent of money in the ground (Matthew 25:14-30). Both hoarding money and ignoring the topic are shirking our responsibility to use what God has given us wisely.

So instead of worrying about having enough in survival mode or becoming dependent on others to fund our lifestyle, **trust God** to provide. God is neither irresponsible nor broke. He hasn't yet created anyone or anything he can't take care of. In Matthew 6:25-33, Jesus reminds us not to worry what we will eat, drink, or wear. Our heavenly Father will provide for us! Notice there's no mention of a three- or five-course buffet nor of the latest *haute couture*. The promise is for food in your tummy and clothes on your back. The preconditions are that you are a child of God, you live righteously, and you pursue his kingdom.

Sometimes, even though you have worked hard, you may find yourself in a **wilderness season**. Like the Israelites, God may have called you out of a familiar place to lead you into an even better place. You are in transition. But the journey involves passing through the wilderness – a place where you can neither sow nor reap. Your sense of security and supplies as you're used to them are gone. Trust that if he is sending you on an errand, he will foot the bill. Like Paul said in 1 Corinthians 9:7, "What soldier has to pay his own expense?" If you're on God's payroll, there's nothing wrong with asking him to provide.

Now, you may be surprised by the unusual means God uses to meet your needs. He fed Elijah with an unclean bird – a raven. He fed the Israelites with manna, a strange food falling from the sky which neither they nor the generations before them had ever seen or known. Don't get stuck on a

DRIVEN BY FEAR OR ANXIETY, WE MAKE POOR FINANCIAL CHOICES.

method God must use – you may miss it if you keep looking for familiar vistas.

And when you're on this journey, just like Jesus told the disciples in Mark 6, don't bother about extra money in your wallet, more clothes than you already have, or the food you'll eat the next day. In Mark 6:9-10, Jesus didn't promise the ones he sent a mansion or seven-star accommodation, but he said they'd be housed. So put your full trust in God.

Now, the wilderness is not all gloom and doom. Sometimes God will throw you a feast to thrill your taste buds and rain down the quail. However, whether manna or meat, the race for survival – what to eat, what to drink, and what to wear – should never distract us from pursuing God's purpose for our lives.

Instead of the traps of survival mode or spending, a healthy relationship with money involves trust in God's provision, working to earn an income, and investing it in God's kingdom. God wants us to be worry-free, and often we find this freedom when we learn to live within our means and be content with what he provides.

FINANCIAL ADVICE

What's worse than being a mature single lady? Being a broke mature single lady! Being broke is definitely not pretty, so let's talk about how to avoid it. We've determined it's OK to talk about and to have money as single ladies. We've talked about how we should approach money. Now, let's talk about how to manage our money wisely.

I understand that we are all at different places in our journeys: those earning a good income, those needing to earn more, those currently without income or seeking new income streams. Since I do not consider myself a financial guru, I would like to share expert advice from Rebecca Obikunle, a financial advisor. From her wealth of experience, she was gracious to share useful tips that will help us manage and grow our finances. The following section is written in her voice, but I will insert my commentary from time to time.

You should earn an income

Everyone needs a source of income. You need to give your services in exchange for money, whether working as an employee, or running a business or a nonprofit that covers its costs. Find something that will keep you busy and earn you an income at the same time. There are many income-generation ideas you can implement without needing a lot of money to start. If you say, "I don't have a job", or "I don't have any business", or "I don't know how to earn", let's look for ideas.

I (Bookie) feel that one of the advantages we have in Africa is the lower barrier to doing business. A lot of us have parents, grandparents, relatives, or neighbours who owned their own businesses. They could range from a kiosk to a large-scale manufacturing plant. Whether it was a stall in the market, a tailoring shop, a carpentry workshop, or even a tray set up in front of their house from which they sold snacks or toiletries, they gained proceeds that enabled them to feed their family, pay for their children and wards' education, and lead reasonably decent lives.

I remember when I was awaiting admission into university, our pastor preached from 2 Thessalonians 3:10, "Those unwilling to work will not get to eat." That really moved me to action! My mum used to buy a drink made from fine millet from her colleague at work. I have yet to find any better *kunu zaki*. It got the nickname *kunumycin* because it was both delicious and nutritious. The lady was kind enough to share her recipe, and my mum was generous to give me a loan of 250 *naira* (less than a dollar). That was all the breakthrough I needed.

It was hard work though! I would trek a long distance to sell it at the biggest secondary school in the area. I was embarrassed when I met students from my neighbourhood

at the school, because I was supposed to be the posh girl who went to a more sophisticated school. I had to cross a major road, carrying a cooler in one hand and a sack in the other. On my way back home, I would stop at the market to buy ingredients for the next supply. Then I would be up at 5 a.m. to deliver orders to my kind neighbour who took gallons of the drink in the boot of his car to sell to his colleagues at work. But I made enough money from that business to contribute towards the family's upkeep and save for when I resumed my first year in the university.

Rebecca says: What's in your hands? Even if you think you are starting from ground zero, God has a way of sorting you out somehow. At your lowest, God might send you someone who will show you kindness, give you a chance, open a door of opportunity for you, or teach you a skill. Be open to what that is and make the best of it.

I like to think of the prophet's widow in 2 Kings 4. Her husband left her with so much debt her sons were in danger of being sold into slavery. But Elisha said, "What can I do to help you?" and "What do you have in the house?" God multiplied the little olive oil she had until it filled every pot she could find – providing her and her sons with enough to pay their debts and provide for themselves.

Even if we don't have money, we often have time and skill. These are usually what we exchange for an income. To increase our ability to learn, we can acquire skills. You may want to start with a "skill-gap analysis". Identify your skills and assets as well as additional skills you'll need to navigate gradually towards your end goal. You may need to ask someone to look at your résumé or "skill bank". Create a personal development plan to acquire the necessary skills.

If these skills would take time to acquire in a more medium- or long-term timeframe, you can start setting money aside to fund this, as may be needed. For the short-term, you can acquire skills that are more easily convertible and can start earning you an income immediately. This could be freelancing, teaching other people things, setting up your own kitchen, learning about affiliate marketing or coaching, or putting your profile online to sell skills and services. Thankfully many resources and trainings are online and some of them are free.

BEING BROKE
IS DEFINITELY
NOT PRETTY.

Creating financial goals

A lady should have financial goals and document them, whether she is married or not. What are the reasons why being financially secure and independent is important for you? Money cannot give you joy and peace and love. But there are some other things money can do for you which are important parts of your life.

Perhaps you want to be able to take care of the bills and not have to knock on people's doors for that. Maybe you want to have goddaughters and be able to lavish on them or even adopt. Do you want to be able to give and support a cause that is dear to your heart or help a friend in need? Give yourself a reason that will motivate you to make changes in your choices.

Having a long-range goal also helps to fine-tune your lifestyle and money habits from here on. For instance, what financial goals would you like to have achieved by the age of 60 or when you retire? Do you want to clear up debt or pay off your mortgage (if applicable)? How many properties, stocks or shares, and life insurance would you like to own? Where are you right now and where would you like to be?

This will help to create a road map for reaching the goals you have already set. It will help you narrow down how much to earn, save, or invest on a monthly basis. When they are broken down, your financial goals become measurable and more achievable. I (Bookie) also recommend that you find a support system – a friend, mentor, coach or accountability partner – to support you through your career and financial goals.

What are your money habits?

According to Rebecca, the next step would be to assess where you are at the moment. What's my income? What things are making money for me? How many streams of income do I have? Do I have passive income coming in?

Once you identify that, look at your outflows. Discover your money *habits*. How do I spend money? What goes out as gifts, as support to my parents and siblings, etc.? How much do I pay in tithe and offering? What percentage of my income goes to my wardrobe, dining out, or social outings? How much do I spend on my health care? Have I been saving or not saving? Have I been investing well?

One of the best ways to determine your outflow and your spending habits is to have a budget. We should always have budgets: a weekly budget, a monthly budget, a quarterly budget, and an annual budget. Having a budget helps us prepare for annual or one-off expenses; for example, if you need to get a certification, travel, get personal development, acquire new skills, give, or cover other unexpected expenses. You can deduct a specific amount or percentage of your income and put it aside.

Budgeting allows us to identify where the big chunks of spending are happening. Unhealthy or impulsive spending habits are often little expenses, but they eventually cut a big hole in our pockets. The big things that take money from you are within your power to change. Where we spend our money reveals our priorities. You can ask: Is this where I want my heart to go? Scripture reminds us that "wherever your treasure is, there the desires of your heart will also be" (Matthew 6:21).

DISCOVER YOUR MONEY HABITS.

When we know where our money is going, Rebecca says we can also ask: Is this sustainable? It depends where you are now and the outcome you wish to achieve. Having a budget also shows us how much income we need to meet our financial goals.

Making a transition

Once you have identified your end goals, you will often be motivated to make a transition. Lots of people are stuck in situations which will not take them to their desired destinations, but they're too scared to step out of there. However, when you look at the big picture, it will help you find the road map of the changes you need to make. It may be getting a new job, starting a new career or business, or even getting out of debt. The next step is to develop an exit strategy to move you from point A to point B. This will involve taking a small step at time to progress towards your goal.

Don't just wake up tomorrow morning and drop your resignation, unless you are convinced God is asking you to do so. Rather, develop a strategy depending on how much time you have (e.g., three months, a year, two years, or even more). Set a date and prayerfully plan what you will be doing between now and the set time to move you towards the next step. The next step may include applying for other jobs or taking a course to equip you for your next line of work or business. Create a backup plan before leaving your current job, business, or schooling.

Often we hold back from taking risks and big steps for fear of how our basic needs will be met without a secure source of income. As you plan for a transition, identify how to make some money to pay basic bills. If you have enough money saved, have you created a plan for how the funds can be best used and not mismanaged? Can you also identify additional sources of income or tested investment vehicles to gain other passive sources of income?

If we have a safety net or assurance of an alternative source of income to fall back on, we are more courageous about taking on opportunities God brings our way. For instance, it was easy to pull out of my job knowing I had savings that could stretch for over a year. I could even pull out of my retirement savings if the need arose.

One advantage of being single is that we can take risks – and even fail and pick ourselves up easily – without jeopardizing those dependent on us for their sustenance. Not taking steps now could mean regrets in the future. You don't want to regret not doing what you could have when you're older and no longer have the strength or opportunities for it. Remember, being undecided is a decision.

BEWARE OF FREELOADERS

Having learned so much from Rebecca's advice, I want to give you a few more pieces of my own advice. One of the beautiful things about our cultures is that we are caring and sharing. We are communal rather than individualistic. Nobody succeeds for themselves alone and no one is supposed to bear their problems alone. We all partake in bits of everyone's success and problems. A lot of us have been beneficiaries of generosity from relatives, neighbours, and even strangers, so we also expect to bless others.

Unfortunately, this can be a precarious situation for single ladies. The premise is usually that a single lady "does not have responsibilities" and so should be able to share her money with all and sundry. Some single ladies are subjected to emotional blackmail by relatives for not taking on the responsibilities of their immediate and extended family. If they are eldest siblings, they are often expected to take this on. Other families may pressure these ladies to at least marry so their husbands will sponsor the family.

A single lady is often an easy target for freeloaders and, if not careful, she will attract a lot of parasitic relationships. In fact, many successful ladies have been duped by preying men who profess love as bait to swindle them out of their money and assets. Not to mention false pastors or religious leaders who cash in on our desperation for marriage and make us part with valuables in exchange for prayers.

Women are generally tender at heart and easily moved by sob stories, so lots of people make up unimaginable tales just to get money out of unsuspecting ladies. Some come with the pretext of seeking soft loans with no intent to repay. While we should be generous and giving, we have to develop the ability to discern between genuine needs and guile. Like my pastor Dr Sam Adeyemi will jokingly say, "If you try to become El-Shaddai (the all sufficient one), you'll eventually become I-shall-die."

Rebecca advises setting aside a budget for giving. She says you shouldn't go into debt because you are trying to help other people. You cannot help everybody. Even Jesus, the great physician, did not heal everyone. In Capernaum, after he healed many people and rebuked many demons, the people didn't want him to leave. Even though there were probably many more needy people, he knew he was sent to preach to the other towns, too, and he moved on (Luke 4:40-44).

You're not sent to save the world. But there are people to whom you are sent. Don't ignore them and spread your resources too thin on other things. God has given you your resources to bless others. But you will give account for what God has given you and the assignment he has for you.

LOOK TO THE ANT

Money is a means of exchange we all need for survival, regardless of gender and marital status. It's a tool we can use to advance God's purposes in his kingdom.

Rebecca likes to say, "Proverbs 6:6-8 encourages us to observe the ant and be wise. Ants have no rank leader, yet they work hard and save during the summer. As a result, they have food to eat even in wintertime when they can no longer work. That is the power of planning and foresight. If the ants can do it without a leader, we can do it without a husband, ladies! We don't have an excuse to wait for a man to put our finances straight or shy away from success for fear of being intimidating. It's our responsibility."

Whatever resources God has committed into our hands, he expects us to be faithful in utilizing them in ways that will please him and bless others. I hope this chapter has given you a good start on the information and education you need to start taking steps towards your financial future.

Happily Ever After Starts Here

Reflections

- What is your mindset about having money as a single lady?

_____

_____

_____

_____

- What have other people told you about being successful and how it might affect your chances of getting married?

_____

_____

_____

_____

- Revisit the money mindsets: spend vs. earn and invest; fear vs. trust. Which ones describe your current relationship with money?

_____

_____

_____

- What is your confidence level when it comes to handling money? Why?

_____

_____

_____

Exercise

- Take stock of where you are now in your finances. Go to https://bit.ly/HWA-BudgetTemplate to download a worksheet and budget template that will guide you through a helpful exercise.

- Goals: Set specific goals about what you would like to achieve in your finances in the long term. Why are these goals important to you? What will they enable you to do?

- Income: Is your current income enough to accomplish your goals? What do you have in your hands that you could use to earn an income? Conduct a skills-gap analysis to see what additional skills you would like to learn or consider what transitions you may want to make to achieve your goals.

- Budget: Create a budget to identify your money habits or review your existing budget and compare it with your actual spending. Consider how much you are giving and saving as well. Does your budget reflect your values and God's priorities? What changes would you like to make?

What the Bible says about money success

Remember the Lord your God. He is the one who gives you power to be successful, in order to fulfil the covenant he confirmed to your ancestors with an oath (Deuteronomy 8:18).

10

"Happily Never After"?

I was catching up with an old friend I hadn't spoken to in a while. She had been married for a long time and had not had a child yet. I couldn't help remembering before she got married, how we would get together and dream. She had very tall dreams.

But now it seemed like the only thing about her life was wanting a child. She had spent so many years pining that not having a child seemed to define her. I was sad that she wasn't living those dreams.

Over the years I had been supportive, counselling and encouraging her. I decided this time to show some tough love: "What if you never have a child? Have you ever thought about that? Can you come to terms and make peace with that?" I admonished her.

As I got off that call, I was still thinking about the conversation and feeling unhappy about my friend's state. All of a sudden, my question swung back at me like a boomerang: "So, what if you never get married?"

I'm not sure I've ever been confronted with a scarier thought. "Wow, wow, wow," I said to myself. "It's so easy to sermonize at other people."

As the years progress, the hope of getting married starts to dim. However, having arrived at this threshold, a lot of people still have many unresolved questions and may not be fully prepared for what may lay ahead.

As a single lady, how do you determine if, like Paul and Jesus, you are called to a life of celibacy? If you should choose or find yourself heading towards a lifetime of singleness, how can you prepare to adapt well and still go on to be truly fulfilled? We'll explore these questions in this chapter.

ASKING THE HARD QUESTIONS

"What if you never get married?" I must confess that I still haven't been able to answer that question without a shudder, but it set me on a mission. I have been asking other single ladies I meet and getting them to contemplate arguably the hardest questions of their lives.

When I asked Zainab, she said, "If it never happens, so be it. That's me speaking more from resignation to fate than thinking through how I will cope, but I have coped all these years. Let's just continue coping."

I inquired further, "But I think there's a difference when there's an end in sight and when there isn't. Nonetheless, I agree it's a journey of a day at a time. At what age would you simply get tired of waiting and decide to embrace the idea that marriage may not happen for you personally?"

"50," she said.

"I had once said 45 when I was in my early 30s. But now that 45 is closer than ever, I think I'll shift the bar further a little."

"Haha. I will be 45 in October and as of this morning I gave up. But when you asked, I said 50, just because!"

I also asked some other friends, "Have you thought about how you could cope with being single until forever?"

Rosemary tells herself she will cope one way or another. "But to be honest, I don't think it will be easy. Special grace will be required. However, let's face it, not everyone will end up following the seemingly ideal path of marriage."

Abiade believes that God gives us desires in accordance with his will: "If it's in the plan for me, it will happen. If not, God will remove the desire for it from me without taking away my joy, fulfilment, and peace."

Some of us will opt for a life of singleness rather than settle for less than what we believe is God's best for us in marriage.

After talking to these friends, I went further to interview some ladies in their early 50s. I have their permission to share their insights about how they are coping or making peace, which I believe will encourage anyone who might be in a similar situation.

JACKIE'S JOURNEY

What would you do if you woke up one morning and realized you were turning 49 and still single? I was introduced to Rev Jackie Othoro from Kenya by my editor, Hannah, and she shared her story.

Like every young lady, Rev Jackie had dreams. Dreams that she would find "the one", get married shortly after university, have children by her mid-30s, and live happily ever after. But when she turned 49, it hit her that it was her last year in her 40s. It wasn't a good year.

She had heard of people getting married for the first time in their 40s, but not as many in their 50s. She told me, "It's almost as if an invisible door was swinging shut. People tell you, 'Well, when you get to your 50s, don't hope to find a man who's never been married. Be prepared for widowers, divorced men, or someone with a couple of baby mamas. He must have had kids.' If you have in your mind a fixed way of understanding what you want for a marriage partner, it begins to shake your foundations."

IT'S A JOURNEY OF A DAY AT A TIME.

It prompted her to do some deep soul-searching. She asked God a lot of questions: "I have done everything right. I have been good. I have stayed pure. I have even served you. This is the one thing I'm asking for."

Rev Jackie says, "I've been very strong for most of my adult life. I know I'm wavering a little bit, but I'm still saying, Lord, please don't put me away."

In an earlier chapter I wrote about finding and pursuing purpose as a single lady. When Rev Jackie reached that crossroad, she started a support group for single ladies aged 35 and above called The Journey. It is open to women who are single and okay with it, as well as those who want to meet someone and have children. The idea is to help each one navigate that tumultuous phase and make peace with their singleness.

"There's a lot of laughter and a bit of tears reflecting on your own life. It's quite an emotional journey to walk with these ladies. We are a small community of women where people figure out some things about themselves and learn to be at peace, saying, 'If we get married, wonderful. If we don't, we're also OK now.' It's called The Journey because the destination may be different for each of us, but it's a journey we all have to take.

"The philosophy I've always lived with is that 'you can't put your life on hold'. Suppose I've got 10, 15, 30 more years to live and I'm going to be single until I'm 80, 90, or even 100. Am I going to be living it or wishing for what hasn't happened yet? Believe me, I have my moments of asking why, but by and large, I think I'd be fine if it didn't happen. I would survive and thrive."

EUGENIA'S CALLING

For Eugenia, hitting 49 was a milestone as well. "You're asking this question at the right time because I made my peace last year. Before that, it was a struggle. I was not married, and I badly wanted to be married.

"I was in an emotionally and verbally abusive relationship. I almost ended up in a violent event that could have cost me my life, but God delivered me in the most remarkable spiritual way.

"Realizing how far I strayed from God's will for my life, I really rededicated myself to Christ. I said, 'Father, you had been showing me the warning signs. I ignored them because I wanted to be married. I stayed in the relationship because I didn't want to disappoint my parents but, God, it is really you I don't want to ever disappoint like this anymore.'"

Eugenia's watchword for her life became *peace*. "I wanted to fight for my peace no matter what. I dove into my relationship with Christ, into the Word, into worship – the things that brought me peace and joy."

However, she realized that her parents and elders in her church were looking at her as if to say, "OK, so you've moved on from that relationship. When is the next one?" As the firstborn, she knew her parents still hoped she would marry. They were praying earnestly for her marriage.

It got to a point where whenever she prayed, she didn't say, "God, where's my husband?" but "God, why are you not answering my mother's prayer? Please, just give them a testimony."

She believes the Holy Spirit brought that to her attention: "You've been asking me to answer your mother's prayer. What is it you want? Are you content?"

She says, "I knew I was content without a doubt. In fact, people noticed this and would gravitate towards me to counsel single women. I felt this strong unction to just let go and let God. I had asked for peace when I had that breakup, and God rewarded my heart with so much contentment."

About a year or two after Eugenia found her peace, her parents brought up the subject of marriage and tried to set her up on a couple of occasions. The pressure became unbearable, so she decided to share with them honestly.

"Mum, Dad, I have something I have to tell you." She told them she had been praying for their prayers to be answered, but marriage was no longer her own prayer for her life. "I felt frustrated because you guys were not happy, and I wanted you to be happy. But it's not right for me to want to be married just to make you happy. I believe God has called me to live a single life until he changes it. I'm at peace with it. I really sense a call from God to be set apart and to live for him."

Her mother's heart broke. "How do you fight against somebody who tells you 'God has said' and that's it? I guess I have to tell the people who fasted, prayed, endured sleepless

"I WANTED TO FIGHT FOR MY PEACE NO MATTER WHAT."

nights, and cried for you. If God has said and that is what you want, we will stop praying."

Her dad was a bit more supportive. "Well, finally now I have an answer. It's hard to know that you cannot expect a grandchild from your firstborn. But I'm glad God has called you to this."

"What about children?" her mum said. "At least have a child."

"Mum, that's not why you marry. People who do that make that child their identity. They place all their hopes and expectations on the child. If God brings me a child for adoption as part of this singleness he's called me to, that's fine. But I'm not going to go get married just to have a child." She was surprised that they were still expecting a miracle at 49.

Her mum asked once more, "Do you feel God has given you a completely closed door?"

"When I prayed about it, I sensed God saying that if the door opens again and he brings me a husband, I will be at peace with that too. But for now, too many people are manipulating and distracting me with that demand. And this is a season where God wants me to be set apart and focus on ministry. I need to be happy even if I never get married. It wasn't a feeling that God forced on me."

Breaking the news to her parents felt terrible – even physically. After their conversation, Eugenia immediately developed a fever and her nose was dripping wet. Although the process was painful, she had known she would pay a price as someone called to an uncommon walk. She advises us, "It doesn't mean you won't break your family's heart. But hopefully they will eventually reconcile with it. They will see you in a new light."

I'm so glad Eugenia demystified how she decided God was calling her to be single, so she could consecrate herself to serve God. The truth is, not everyone will be married. This is not for everybody, but if you know this is for you, then like Jesus said, receive it and receive the grace for it (Matthew 19:12).

If God has called you to a life of singleness, he backs it up with his peace. The journey still won't be easy. People close to you might question your choice and continue to put pressure on you. While they may never come around to accepting it, you have to stick to your conviction and stay focused on the race to which God is calling you.

JULIAN'S STORY

Pondering upon a lifetime of singlehood does not necessarily mean you do not have faith in God or that you have given up on marriage. As Julian approached 40, she decided marriage was probably not for her. She had been told nobody would marry her type.

She is totally non-traditional. I remember watching a video of her thanksgiving celebration in church when she turned 40 and thinking, "Wow, what 40-year-old lady does a church celebration when she is single?" People had labelled her a rebel because she didn't seem to care so much about getting married. What drew me was how she lived her life to the fullest as a single lady. She was very confident, vibrant, zestful, and had an excellent touch to everything she did.

Julian had seen enough dysfunctional marriages to make marriage look like a disincentive to a free spirit like herself. Upon making that decision, she sat down to take stock: what would she miss if she never got married? Maybe sex and physical intimacy?

She went to God and prayed he would take away all sexual urges from her. She wanted to be free to live celibately and single for the rest of her life. This gave her peace of mind to focus on her God-given assignment.

Just after she had settled this in her mind and wasn't looking, a man showed up. He ticked all her boxes for what she wanted but didn't think could exist. Today, Julian has one of the most enviable marriages with a man as unconventional as herself. A match made in heaven, you would say!

I decided to share a "happily ever after" story last just to point out that contemplating a lifetime of singlehood doesn't mean you will end up single for ever any more than writing a will means you will die anytime soon. Similar to death, a lifetime of singleness is a topic we would rather not talk about. It holds so much trepidation for us. Perhaps the only way to disarm that dread is to confront and demystify it. Then if marriage eventually happens, we're happy. If it doesn't, we're no worse off because we already thought this through and prepared for it. Sometimes, the greatest miracle that can happen to us is not our circumstances changing, but our perspectives of the situation changing.

WHAT ABOUT MARRIAGE WILL YOU MISS?

Julian asked herself, "What would I miss if I never got married?" I decided to ask the ladies I was interviewing the same question.

Jackie said, "At this point, I have come to terms with being single for the rest of my life. However, I realized that at this stage you just want companionship, someone to grow old with into your 50s, 60s, or 70s.

"We want to have someone we can travel with, someone we can grow old with, someone we can just be silent with in the house. You go home, and the whole house is dark and empty because there's nobody at all until you switch on the lights. When you grow older, your circle of friends also shrinks. You don't even have the capacity to have so many people around.

"Another facet of companionship I'd miss is someone to challenge my mind. The kind of person that would push me to keep going and get better. They would know me so well and cheer me on to be so much more, 'Come on, you're a champion. You count. You can do better.' At the same time, they can slow you down and say, 'Ok, that is foolish thinking.'"

Eugenia, on the other hand, didn't seem to be missing companionship. "I don't desire to mingle my life with anybody right now. It's hard for people to understand how you're not lonely, but I'm not because I believe that is a unique anointing." Being single and content means being at peace with aloneness, but not necessarily loneliness.

Another important aspect of life-long singleness that could be a bother is sex, especially for anyone who has decided not to indulge outside of marriage. According to Jackie, "Many of us don't want to talk about it, but the other thing we'd miss is just the physical aspect of sex." I agree.

During a discussion in a Christian group for women, we were talking about being content as a single. I raised this question: "Yes, I know God is all I need and is able to meet all my needs, but God can't meet my sexual needs. That is a very valid desire that should only be met in marriage. So, how in God can we meet this need as single Christian women?"

We discussed in the earlier chapters the value of finding community and devoting ourselves to sexual purity. I also decided to ask Eugenia her thoughts. She said, "Some questions won't have a comfortable answer. According to Paul, if you cannot control yourself, then you should marry, for it is better to marry than to burn with passion (1 Corinthians 7:9). If you're called to be single, God will give you the grace to live a single life with integrity. Your sexual desire will dampen substantially.

"In my early 40s, I prayed about it and said, 'Lord, if you don't want me to get married, then take care of this.' For many women, desire could be age-related. At a younger age, your hormonal urge will still be high, but as you get older, it wanes. I have also noticed that sexual desire is not an issue as I get older, as my focus and energies have shifted strongly toward spiritual matters and other aspects of living."

I once listened to a woman of God that I respect so much talk about when she was in her late 40s and unmarried. She was lamenting to God, "I don't have this, and I don't have that." God replied to her, "But you have me." It was true from my perspective that she had an enviable, intimate relationship with God. Having come this far with a lot still unaccomplished in my life, I have held this close to my heart over the years. I keep turning it over in my mind, measuring it against the situations, and weighing them to see if having God is actually truly enough.

I can categorically and authoritatively say that God has been enough and more than enough. I may not have everything I wanted when I wanted it, but I still know that God loves me. Just look at this Scripture passage:

> But now, God's Message,
> the God who made you in the first place, Jacob,
> the One who got you started, Israel:
> "Don't be afraid, I've redeemed you.
> I've called your name. You're mine.
> When you're in over your head, I'll be there with you.
> When you're in rough waters, you will not
> go down.
> When you're between a rock and a hard place,
> it won't be a dead end –
> Because I am God, your personal God,
> The Holy of Israel, your Saviour.
> I paid a huge price for you:
> all of Egypt, with rich Cush and Seba thrown in!
> *That's* how much you mean to me!
> *That's* how much I love you!
> I'd sell off the whole world to get you back,
> trade the creation just for you
> (Isaiah 43:1-4 MSG).

When we know how much God loves us, we can trust he's got good plans for us – even when we don't see the full picture. For Eugenia, an anchor Scripture has been Proverbs 3:5-6. As she paraphrases it, "If you're trusting God with all your heart, number one, and you're acknowledging him in all your ways, then trust that he's directing your path."

She says, "If he has you on the path of being at peace with being alone, then ask him what purpose he wants in this season and fulfil that purpose. It doesn't always mean life on a stage or any kind of fame. It could just be that he wants you to pour into certain people, because this life on Earth is not forever. We are sowing kingdom seeds for eternity. You have no idea how great of an impact that seed is going to make in that person's life for eternity and for many more people."

WHAT ABOUT SINGLENESS WOULD WE MISS?

Sometimes the grass is greener on the other side, so I decided to also explore another question: What benefits does the single life give us that we might miss if we got married? Could it be that we were idealizing marriage in some respects?

So I interviewed a woman who got married in her 40s. Having been on both sides of the divide, she says, "Single ladies have the illusion that this man will come and make my life perfect. Everything will just be smooth and just wonderful. But a change in your status or title does not automatically produce 'happily ever after'. Marriage is just another different phase.

"Marriage is not picking up another ball and continuing to juggle. It's a different ball game. I actually had to put all the balls down and then choose again which ones I was going to pick up this time. Marriage comes with its own expectations and demands that require some adjustment. Having to wait to be married has also helped me to manage my expectations now that I am waiting to have kids.

"Both sides are good. While I miss my independence and freedom, I'm glad to have someone to depend upon." She reminds us, "Your life won't be defined when you get married. It will just be defined differently. Your life is already defined as the person you are. Your life is complete now, and it would be complete differently if you were married."

Perhaps we would miss the opportunities, independence, and freedom of the single life. Even before Rev Jackie's crisis at

49, she remembers a moment when she turned 30. She decided her life would never go on hold waiting for marriage. Marriage was never clearly promised or given to her, she reasoned, and she had seen the tragedy of people waiting for a man or woman to come into their life before they could do certain things. She wasn't going to miss out on life. "If there were opportunities available for me, I would take them. If there was work that needed to be done, I would happily do it."

> **CONTEMPLATING A SINGLE LIFE DOESN'T MEAN YOU WILL END UP SINGLE FOR EVER.**

For one thing, Rev Jackie has taken advantage of her liberty to travel the world. One day, she's off to the UK; the next, she's in South Africa; and right after that, she's in the US. A friend of hers who got married right after college once said to her, "I really envy you. You're living your life on your terms. I can't do that. I can't just pack up my bag and leave my children and husband. I never had the in-between time to figure out who I was."

It's interesting how everyone tends to look at the other side and think the others have it better! But really, it's just different. It's a good reminder to enjoy your life now.

PONDERING THE POSSIBILITY

Like Rev Jackie's experience and mine, the thought of a lifetime of singleness might feel like a near nightmare at first. But from listening to single women a little bit ahead of me, they start to make peace with what seems like an inevitable lifetime of singleness. Some do this out of resignation, and others out of conviction.

The reality is that some people will not be married as soon as they wish and others will never be married. Pondering the possibility is not intended to dampen your spirit nor is it a sign that you lack faith. Rather, it is a chance to realistically prepare for possible outcomes, consider practical ways to fill any voids that might be left, and find peace.

A lifetime of singleness should not deter us from living our best lives. On the contrary, it could present us with opportunities that might otherwise not be available if we were married. I honestly don't assume it's going to be an easy route. However, confronting our fears headlong rather than shrinking away from them can disarm them. It can give us the confidence and courage to thrive no matter what comes. Then if marriage happens, it's a plus.

Happily Ever After Starts Here

Reflections

- Has it ever crossed your mind that maybe marriage might not happen for you? What was your reaction to that thought?

_____
_____
_____
_____

- Have you tried to picture what a lifelong singleness would look like for you?

_____
_____
_____

- What would be missing in your life if marriage were delayed longer or never happened?

_____
_____
_____

- How could you cope if you had to remain single for much longer than you imagined?

_____

_____

_____

_____

Exercise:

- Take some time to contemplate what the possibilities would be for you to live a fulfilled life even if marriage were not to happen. What could you do to fill gaps that might leave in your life?

_____

_____

_____

_____

_____

- If you happen to know of other godly single ladies willing to discuss with you, consider talking with them about how they are coping too.

What the Bible says about a lifetime of singleness

"Not everyone can accept this statement," Jesus said. "Only those whom God helps. Some are born as eunuchs, some have been made eunuchs by others, and some choose not to marry for the sake of the Kingdom of Heaven. Let anyone accept this who can" (Matthew 19:11-12).

11

Singlehood and Motherhood?

The idea of having and raising children has been ingrained in us since we were little girls, especially as women raised in African settings. I remember having my own little blue plastic doll. I'm sure lots of ladies who are about my age probably had a similar doll.

It wasn't unusual that we would bathe them, dress them up, pretend to feed and even breastfeed them, pet them, cradle them, sing to them, and strap them to our backs, just like we watched our own mother or other mothers do with their babies. Since we were children, we have role-played and practiced to be mothers. It is not likely that instinct in us would go away.

So it makes sense that even after making peace with being single, the question of children can still remain. Rev Jackie said, "The question that I am wrestling with more than the husband issue is the child issue. I always knew I wanted to be a mother. I think I'd make an awesome mother. I've mentored teenage girls into young adulthood. If I never have biological children, would that mean I never become a mother? I'm talking about a biological mother as opposed to a spiritual mother."

In my conversations with a number of older single ladies, I realize that having a child is becoming a popular option for moving on. They don't want to put their lives on hold while waiting for marriage, and it seems to give some sense of closure to the elusive "happily ever after". The rationale, I believe, can be summarized as, "Well, I don't have control over a man marrying me, but maybe I could focus on something within my control. If I can't have a man, then I might as well have a child I can call mine."

So, what are our options as single Christian women when it comes to having children?

ADOPTION

Recently, I attended a seminar on parenting options. One of the speakers was Joke Silva, a renowned veteran actress and Christian woman, who herself was adopted and never met her biological parents. I would like to share some of the things I gleaned from her and other speakers on adoption, then take it a notch further by tailoring the discussion to single ladies.

For Joke Silva, the purpose for adoption is: "I want to share my love through this human who didn't come from my womb but is a child of my heart." In deciding for adoption, we should realize that a child is a gift and every gift from God is good. A real parent is not necessarily the one who births a child, but the one who works with God to raise a child and bring them into their destiny. Love is more powerful than genes.

I wish to highlight another set of hard questions to help us adequately prepare should we pursue adoption as single ladies.

Age

What age of child are you looking for? An infant would require more attention, changing diapers, sleepless nights, and fatigue, but there is more likelihood that you would be able to bond with the baby and be there through different stages of growth. An older child would be more independent, but perhaps would have also developed some habits and potentially have had more time to accumulate trauma. However, you might be more similar in age to the parents of your child's agemates if you adopted an older child.

The child's history

Even biological parenting comes with its own risks. When you adopt, there is the added difficulty that you often don't have a lot of information about the child's birth parents or family background to understand potential risks or history. You might discover congenital issues, trauma, or other unexpected matters.

It is also good to envision and plan how you will respond to the child asking why they don't have a father, whether and when you will tell them they are adopted, and how you will handle questions about or the desire to reconnect with their biological parents.

Resources and support

As a single parent, it's important to know what resources and help you have available. Do you have a support system to help you cope, such as family, friends, and neighbours? For instance, Jackie says she contemplated adoption when she was in her mid-40s. But she decided, "I don't want to do this alone. I want to parent a child with a husband because a child just needs an amazing man in their life. There's just something about bringing up a child in the context of a marriage, which was what kept me away from adopting."

Ask yourself whether you have the resources you will need: financial, spiritual, emotional, and time. Consider too that legislation in many African countries makes adoption quite prohibitive, as single women may be discriminated against. It is wise to be prepared for the journey.

Community attitude

What is your family and community's attitude? In Nigeria, there is a strong stigma against adopted children. Joke Silva's first relationship ended because the man said his family wouldn't accept an adoptee. There is a risk that your family members will see them as "less" than other children in the family. They might also be opposed because they believe it will further reduce your chances of being married. If the child has to cope with stigmas and labels from friends, neighbours, and even family members, how will you deal with that?

Although some people and cultures frown on adoption, remember that God also adopted us into his family. Ephesians 1:4-7 says:

> Even before he made the world, God loved us and chose us in Christ to be holy and without fault in his eyes. God decided in advance to adopt us into his own family by bringing us to himself through Jesus Christ. This is what he wanted to do, and it gave him great pleasure. So we praise God for the glorious grace he has poured out on us who belong to his dear Son. He is so rich in kindness and grace that he purchased our freedom with the blood of his Son and forgave our sins.

Verses like these show us that the decision to adopt reflects the heart of God as a Father. God wants all of his creation on earth to experience a taste of his loving parent heart. God is the "Father to the fatherless, defender of widows . . . God places the lonely in families" (Psalm 68:5-6). When we take in orphans, we become the vessels through which they experience God's love which they might otherwise not have.

FOSTERING

My friend Toyin says, "From my view as a pragmatic person, perhaps while waiting, I feel people can adopt a child or become a foster mother to children you can support to raise.

Doing this sometimes takes boredom and loneliness away, and gives a sense of fulfilment. I have a friend nearing 45 who told me she has lost those unfulfilled feelings ever since she accepted training three of her poor relatives. One has grown, graduated, and got married under her parenting."

Toyin's comment points out that while legal adoption is less common in our contexts, informal adoption by raising the child of a family member or fostering an abandoned child from the community is quite common. The role of an *auntie* can often look very similar to that of a mother, even raising a child in one's home for several years. The fostering route can cut out some of the issues with formal adoption but can have its own challenges.

You know the family the child is from. This can address a concern many people have about the child coming from a family with a history of mental illness or undetected congenital diseases. It also takes away the attendant stress of the process of legal adoption, as parents or guardians of the child willingly give them to people they know and can trust.

Fostering is also well embraced and looked on favourably in our cultures, which can reduce stigma. Women who informally adopt and raise children that are not theirs are held in high esteem, respected, and seen as responsible. Society easily overlooks the fact that they are not married and don't have biological children.

BLESSING OTHERS BRINGS BLESSING.

Since the woman is also seen as now responsible, there might be less financial burden or demands on her from freeloaders, who otherwise would see her as a person without obligations. This way, she is also able to channel her investments into giving a child a good life, rather than respond to every demand from relatives. However, being a single parent is still a huge investment, and the same questions of one's support systems and resources apply to fostering as to adoption.

There are also a few unique challenges with fostering. If the child's family is still around, they may become freeloaders. They can become manipulative in requesting you to do more favours for them in addition to raising the child. The child may also be older than in many adoption situations and come with more baggage that you have to deal with. As with any parenting option, consider the pros and cons carefully before reaching a decision.

With both methods of parenting, Toyin says, "You can become a source of blessing to others. There are orphans all around, children of poor families whom we can raise up and improve their circumstances and prospects. It is not absolutely necessary that you should only care for children of your womb. Let's start to impact our world."

FOSTERING IS ALSO WELL EMBRACED AND LOOKED ON FAVOURABLY IN OUR CULTURES.

Often, blessing others brings blessing. There are stories of how such adoptive parents have been taken care of in old age by children they raised. A popular saying in Yoruba is, "It is the person who had children to bury them that gave birth, not necessarily the one who had biological children."

HAVING BIOLOGICAL CHILDREN

Another parenting option some people consider is pregnancy outside of marriage. There are many women who decide to have a child by a man they are not married to. This could be because they cannot stand the pressure, they want to be independent of a man, or they decide they are getting too old and need to use any means possible to have a baby. We have talked in a previous chapter about how sex outside of marriage is explicitly not approved in the Bible. I don't mean to condemn or judge people who have gone this route as a matter of choice or error. But if we have decided to make

God's Word the final authority in our lives, I don't believe this is an option for us as God's children.

These days, some people pursue pregnancy through artificial methods. A few examples of this are artificial insemination, e.g., intrauterine insemination (IUI) and in vitro fertilization (IVF). These methods assist fertilization of a woman's eggs either inside her womb or in a lab, and then she carries the child in her womb.

This idea can be attractive to some women because the child will have some of her DNA, and she will go through the whole process from pregnancy. However, it can be very expensive financially and can also be quite taxing emotionally and physically. Success rates are also quite low. According to WebMD, "a woman who is under age 35 and undergoes IVF has a 39.6 per cent chance of having a baby, while a woman over age 40 has an 11.5 per cent chance."[6]

For married couples, the husband's sperm is used. However, single women would need to find a sperm donor. Of course, a woman who has a child out of wedlock has some explaining to do to her community, since we only know of one immaculate conception. The assumption of being promiscuous is an additional stigma on top of already being a single woman. But is this merely prejudice, or are there theological reasons why this is looked down on for single Christian ladies?

One major argument against artificial methods of pregnancy for single women is that when God gave the original command to be fruitful and multiply, it involved a man and woman becoming one flesh. When married couples pursue IVF, the child is conceived in a marriage union.

However, single women who conceive using sperm donors may not be having sex outside of marriage, but they are still becoming one flesh with someone who is not their husband. They aren't conceiving a child within the context of a marriage union as God intended. Choosing to get pregnant without

---

6 "Infertility and In Vitro Fertilization," *Webmd.com,* 1 August 2021, https://www.webmd.com/infertility-and-reproduction/guide/in-vitro-fertilization#1.

a man in the child's life separates the union God intended between men and women. While single mothers face the unfortunate reality of bringing up children without the child's father, it isn't the route we should deliberately choose to pursue as Christians. While adoption has strong biblical support, we don't see the same for pregnancy outside of wedlock, even by artificial methods.

For anyone considering the route of single parenting, I hope this section has helped you to have more information about the decision and to be aware of the need for thorough preparation.

INVEST IN THE NEXT GENERATION

Even if we don't have children, we can gain some of that same fulfilment by mentoring children and younger people. It is also a way we can effectively serve God. As young people start getting introduced to the real world, they are constantly faced with intense peer pressures – fear of the future, choices to make for their career, questions about God and morality, and hypocrisy from respected adults. It's a delicate phase of their lives. They are looking for examples, and the person who gets their ears and hearts will greatly influence the course of their lives. They need guidance, words of encouragement, and someone believing in them to become all God created them to be.

You can be that person. Like parenting, no special qualifications are required. They can learn from your failures as much as successes. Like a proverb says, "A child may have more clothes, but can never have as many worn or ragged ones as an elderly one." Your experience has equipped you to guide younger people and prepare them for the future.

God can transform the lives of others through us when we cooperate with him to mentor and influence young people around us. I will never forget a teacher in my elementary school; the way she modelled Christ made him so real. She had sown the seed, and God led a harvester on the street corner to hand me a Christian tract on my way from school. To an observer it might have seemed a waste giving an eight-year-old a tract, but the evangelist did not despise me for being a child. So it was that I gave my life to Christ without anyone preaching to me and though my family did not belong to any local assembly.

In high school, my literature teacher took a chance on me. She let me into her class on trial even though I had missed a whole year of coursework. About a year later I missed one of her classes and she noticed, in a combined class of over 70 people. When she sent for me, I was afraid that I was in trouble, but she spoke very kindly to me and made me promise to do my best in the subject. I had never felt so affirmed by a teacher.

SHE SAW SOMETHING I DIDN'T SEE IN MYSELF.

I eventually had the highest grade possible in that subject, although it was not my major, because I loved her and couldn't afford to disappoint her. As I write this, my third book, more than 25 years later, I can't help but be grateful that she saw something I didn't see in myself. These are the kinds of impact we can have when we invest in the next generation.

While I don't have children, one of the greatest fulfilments of my adult life has been mentoring young people in my local community. After my university education, I moved back home. I saw lots of youth helpless, hapless, and lost. Their futures seemed bleak with no hope of getting tertiary education. I was moved to do something about it.

Using my platform as a house fellowship leader in church, I started to train young people closest to me in the community. Together with these youth leaders, we organized outreaches and re-orientation seminars for other youths in the community, held similar programmes in schools, produced a quarterly publication which provided career guidance, and organized free tutorials for those preparing for university qualifying examinations. We also went from house to house to engage the parents and guardians of the youth. It was my greatest delight to see a lot of the youth get into universities and colleges. Today, a lot of them have families of their own, have built businesses, have thriving careers, and some are in ministry.

Many years later after I thought I had hung my boots, I met another young man at a grocery store in a new neighbourhood I had just moved to. He had suffered rejection by close family members and needed a sense of belonging. I noticed how brilliant, hardworking, and dedicated he was to his work. He also desperately wanted to get higher education but could not afford it on the meagre income he earned.

Although I was not in a good place financially and in my health, I couldn't resist investing in him. I had to do a lot of work helping him gain back his confidence. He eventually got into school, and when I could no longer afford it, God raised people to sponsor his education. He recently finished his final exams and has maintained good grades throughout school.

The day I was leaving Nigeria, he was there to help pack my stuff and clean the house. He called me aside saying, "I'd like to see you." I jokingly reminded him that I was not invisible. But I knew he meant he wanted to see me in private. He spent the next couple of minutes expressing so much gratitude. For the first time since I started preparing for my move, I got so emotional and cried. He had become family to me, and it hurt to feel I was leaving my family behind. I am proud of the great gentleman he has become.

While waiting to have our own biological children, we can allow God to use us to raise spiritual children, as an investment that will be credited to our accounts in eternity. I believe this calling is very dear to the heart of God. Jesus asks us to bring the children to him. Our lives and example will influence them and give them a head start in their knowledge of and walk with God.

As women, we are compassionate and we have the ability to comfort, provide clarity, and to nurture God's deposit in the younger generation. Some of us may have a deep desire for our own children. Based on the analysis I've provided in the chapter, I believe adoption is a wonderful way to express

JESUS ASKS US TO BRING THE CHILDREN TO HIM.

God's loving heart and has good biblical support.

In situations where this might be difficult, you could consider taking responsibility for a child or young person in your community who might be lacking parental care. This could be a more formal arrangement like fostering, or a more casual situation like investing in younger family members or groups of young people in your community.

Even if we don't become a parent, we can still experience many of the joys of motherhood as we seek avenues to pour ourselves into vulnerable children and young people God brings into our lives. If we have a strong desire to have children, we will need to lean on God and ask him for grace for our situations.

Happily Ever After Starts Here

Reflections

- Have you ever considered options for parenting as a single?

_____

_____

- If you have a preferred parenting option, what are the pros and cons that you have considered?

_____

_____

_____

_____

189

- Apart from single parenting, what are some ways you could invest in the next generation?

_____

_____

_____

_____

_____

Exercise

- If you would like to explore any of these parenting situations further, consider talking with people who have adopted or fostered and asking them about their experience. How does this impact your view of the pros and cons of this choice?
- To celebrate the family God has given you – parents, siblings, relatives, nieces, nephews, and friends – create a photo album or a display somewhere you will see regularly. This should also include pictures of younger people who you have invested in.

What the Bible says about families

Father to the fatherless, defender of widows –
  this is God, whose dwelling is holy.
God places the lonely in families;
  he sets the prisoners free and gives them joy
  (Psalm 68:5-6a).

12

Singlehood and God's Fatherhood

I had been trusting God for a business deal I had been eagerly looking forward to for a while, but it fell through at the last minute! I was so disappointed that God didn't grant my request. It seemed he was really being unfair to me. Why was he denying me almost everything I wanted? Wasn't it bad enough that I was not married? Shouldn't I be compensated in some other ways? Or was he just totally out to humiliate me?

Have you ever wondered why, if God really had good plans for your life, he hasn't sorted you out with a husband by now? Sometimes we begin to suspect he's withholding gifts from us for no reason. Our trust issues creep up and it's so easy to become bitter!

I had been grumbling all morning and did not mince words in letting God know how hurt I was feeling. "God, you mind your business and I'll mind mine," I said. It was official – we were not talking.

I got to the office and began racing against time to finish a very important project. It would require the *grace of God* for me to meet the deadline. But, oh, I forgot we were not on talking terms! So I decided

WHEN GOD IS SILENT, IT DOESN'T MEAN HE IS ABSENT.

to turn off my phone to avoid distractions. I soon turned it on again to make a quick call. Just then my brother's call came in. I was very excited to hear from him. After his call, this dialogue started in my mind:

"I thought you were not supposed to take phone calls."

"No, this one is different."

"Why?"

"It's my brother. Not only is his call not a distraction, but I'm actually delighted to take his call anytime."

"Well, that's the way your call is so important and special to me. I am never too busy to listen to you. I never shrug off your requests; I attend to every one of them."

Now wait, that was the Holy Spirit speaking!

Just imagine, I was holding a grudge against God, and he wasn't even mad at me. Rather, he took pains to talk to me because he cares about the way I feel. This was so humbling for me that my eyes filled with tears. I learned a vital lesson: when God is silent, it doesn't mean he is absent. When we can't see his acts, we should trust his heart, for his thoughts concerning us are continually good.

At times, I wonder why God bothers to respond to my rants and whims. Why does he bother with me at all, knowing I can be so silly? David must have felt this way as he reminisced about God's love in Psalm 8:3-4:

> When I look at the night sky and see the work of your
>   fingers –
> the moon and the stars you set in place –
> what are mere mortals that you should think about them,
>   human beings that you should care for them?

Wow! This must have come from a depth of revelation of experiencing God's love and friendship which surpasses any other. My heart overflows with joy to think how much God loves me. While we have been talking about looking for a lover, in this chapter I want to remind us of how loved we are already, by the ultimate Lover of our souls.

THE ULTIMATE SOURCE OF LOVE

While we seek to find love in a soul mate, there are ways that a man's love will always be insufficient. We develop relationships along the way, but no one else will be there for every one of our waking moments – from when we take our first breath until our last. Even our parents, much as they love us, can't always be there. Even mothers who carry a child in their womb for nine months and go through great pain to give birth sometimes still abandon their babies. Spouses profess unconditional love and vow to care for the other through sickness and pain. But sometimes they leave when the vicissitudes of life show up.

Once, I had to be upfront with a friend who so desperately wanted to be married to fill a void in her heart. I let her know that it could damage her even further to get into a marriage with the wrong person out of her desperation for affirmation. Rather than go from relationship to relationship to fill that kind of void, we should invest in building our relationship with God.

For several years, one of my pastors shared how she felt lonely in the early days of her marriage. It made her seek God until she found an intimate relationship with him. This hit home for me recently. Only the love of God can truly fill the void in our hearts. So we must prioritize cultivating an intimate love relationship with God above any earthly relationship. Our relationship with God is the only one that will count, not only in this life but through eternity. So it's just good judgement to invest in your relationship with him!

A MAN'S LOVE WILL ALWAYS BE INSUFFICIENT.

Now, marriage and God's love aren't opposed. I believe God wants his daughters to have happy marriages where they can experience his love expressed through another human.

God designed marriage as one way he wants to model his love. But it will always be an incomplete picture of the depth of God's love. The truth is, when you've had a taste of God's lavish love, it raises the bar because you begin to understand how God really intends for you to be loved and treated in marriage, although you'll never get that level from a fallible human spouse.

FRIGHTENING FATHERS

Some of us have a difficult time grasping how much God loves us because our perspective of God is marred. When we hear that God is our Father, we might think of a typical image of an African father. In our culture, men are often socialized to not express emotions in order to come across as strong and always in charge. It is thought that raising a child is the woman's job, so a father's involvement in his children's lives is often perfunctory at best. The irony is that when a child turns out bad, he is considered as belonging to the mother, while the good child belongs to the father.

The man's role is seen primarily as disciplining and providing. I've heard and read a lot of people's accounts of how as children, once they heard their dad's car coming home, they scampered for safety as they were sure to get into trouble for no reason at all. Like someone humorously said, dads were the "lion of the tribe of their houses".

GOD IS NOT MAD AT YOU!

Even when it came to your father providing, you had to pass your requests through your mother, who had to find a right time when the man was in a good mood to present the request to him. Many of us walked on eggshells around our fathers, and so it's easy to project this same image onto God.

Churches have also played a big role in indoctrinating us wrongly. Religion has painted to us a picture of a vindictive and temperamental God who is only out to punish us for every little misstep we commit. We have been told not to question or query God – it seemed that would emasculate him or defy his authority. We feared we would be severely punished for such audacity. So, a lot of us go around with questions in our heart, feelings of injustice, and pent-up anger. We're just afraid of expressing ourselves and our emotions to God for fear we will rouse the hornet's nest and the unthinkable may happen to us.

But I want to assure you, God is not mad at you! I urge you to forget what you've heard about God wanting to destroy you or that you can't question him. Even when Adam and Eve sinned, God still clothed them. When Cain murdered his brother, God still put a mark of protection on him so that no one would harm him.

Remember, when Jesus was killed, he took the full weight of God's judgement that was meant for us. But Jesus was a human who was also God, so he was able to resist the temptation of sin. Since he never deserved God's punishment, it couldn't hold him down. He conquered sin and death and rose to life again. God is not angry with humanity, because Jesus took the Father's wrath that was caused by sin.

So find God for yourself. Dare to ask him questions. Pour out your anger and frustrations. David did this over and over through the Psalms; Jacob wrestled with an angel; Jonah didn't hide his anger at God; Job did not hold back when he thought God was unfair and heavy-handed. God didn't destroy any of them. Rather, he gave them answers and he blessed them.

AN APPROACHABLE GOD

Now, I don't mean to downplay the sovereignty and almightiness of God. He is indeed fearsome and like the Bible says, "he lives in light so brilliant that no human can approach him" (1 Timothy 6:16). But we can take this reverence too far and let it create unnecessary distance between ourselves and God.

Some time back, I was at the airport to see someone off. I ran into my senior pastor's personal assistant, who had come to receive the pastor returning from a trip. The assistant asked if I had come with my car. The driver who was supposed to pick the pastor up had not arrived. The assistant did not want to hire a taxi, and there were no cab hailing services those days. He wondered if I wouldn't mind dropping the pastor off at his house. Wow, what an honour to offer that service to the pastor! I found it hard to say no.

However, I suddenly became aware of everything that was wrong with my car. It was a small Nissan Sunny with broken air-conditioning. I didn't think it befitting for a man of his calibre. Now, the pastor is one of the simplest African men of God I have known. He has no personal driver, no airs, and a lavish sense of humour. But I still felt as if his presence would suck up all the oxygen in my little jalopy. Fortunately for my racing heart, the driver eventually showed up and I didn't have to do the trip.

KNOWING GOD AS A LOVING FATHER CHANGES HOW WE SPEAK WITH HIM.

In the same way as I reacted to the pastor, some of us try to hide or run away from God because we feel he's too much for us. His presence makes us self-conscious of our own shortfalls and inadequacies. Just like Peter when he encountered Jesus, our reaction is, "Depart from me for I am sinful" (see Luke 5:8). It is true that we are sinful and that we will never be good enough for a holy God on our own strength. Yet there is a way for us to approach him.

The problem comes when we try to be accepted by God through our own righteousness, merits, and good works; and that already disqualifies us. Instead, our qualification is what Christ did already on the cross. Jesus came to give us direct access to God the Father. Because Christ's work is already finished, we're qualified to come to God just as we are. We approach him only on the premise of what Christ did, not what we did or have ever done – right or wrong.

Our acceptance isn't based on our performance but on our family relationship. As Romans 8:15 says, "So you have not received a spirit that makes you fearful slaves. Instead, you received God's Spirit when he adopted you as his own children. Now we call him, '*Abba*, Father'" (emphasis mine). *Abba* is like saying "Daddy!"

Knowing God as a loving Father changes how we speak with him. It gives us confidence. Before he died, Jesus said, "At that time, you won't need to ask me for anything. I tell you the truth, you will ask the Father directly, and he will grant your request because you use my name" (John 16:23). That time is now! I like how the Message version puts it:

> "The world is full of so-called prayer warriors who are prayer-ignorant. They're full of formulas and programs and advice, peddling techniques for getting what you want from God. Don't fall for that nonsense. This is your Father you're dealing with, and he knows better than you what you need" (Matthew 6:7-9 MSG).

A GENTLE FATHER

Let me share a beautiful story that greatly impacted my image of God as a Father. At one Sunday service, I sat in the auditorium for parents with infants. While the service was on, I noticed how a lot of the children made their parents "famous". I mean, if you have to walk to the podium and in front of the congregation while the service is on and you are not the preacher, then you've become a public figure of sorts.

I spotted a tiny little girl about a year old in a pink dress. She kept wandering to the front of the podium. Her father, a six-feet-plus, bespectacled man, stooped down to hold his daughter's hand and walked her back to their seats. He'd whisper something in her ear, I guess admonishing her not to go back, but no sooner than he'd managed to get her to their seats, she would be off again in her wanderlust.

It must have happened close to 10 times in the duration of the service. It started to look ridiculous. I wondered why he didn't let her go. Why was he bothering so much since she was bent on doing her own thing? She wasn't going to heed his warning anyway; she was too young to comprehend the dangers of going off on her own. Perhaps, I thought, he could just strap her up so she would be forced to stay in one place.

The next time I saw little princess in pink, she had crossed to the other half of the auditorium. In no time, daddy had gone after her. He seemed more determined. This time, he did not lead her by the hand. He carried her and held her firm in his arms.

And that was the last time the little Miss Pink went straying.

That little scene ministered the Father heart of God to me. When I stray, I'm so glad God doesn't give up on coming after me. He lovingly stoops to my level and leads me to my rightful place beside him. No matter how obstinate I am, his love is always more persistent.

EVEN WHEN WE ARE UNFAITHFUL

Perhaps you think you're an exception; God couldn't love you like that. Maybe you even think your singleness is a result of a sin. You might have a past you're not so proud of, you may have been in relationships you should never have, or you may have done things you shouldn't have. This may have made you believe that you don't deserve to be married or that you have to undo your sinful past in order to be marriage-worthy. That is a lie from the Devil – and perhaps from other people he is using to sell this lie to you.

I particularly love the first chapter of the book of Matthew, which outlines Jesus's ancestry. While in the Jewish culture, genealogy is read through the patriarchal line, we see this pattern interrupted a few times. Against the norm, women such as Tamar, Rahab, Ruth, Bathsheba, and Mary are featured in Jesus's family tree.

What's even more interesting with this seeming anomaly is that if you take a closer look at these women, they had stains in their stories. After Tamar was widowed twice and still childless, she dressed like a prostitute to get a son with her father-in-law. Rahab was a prostitute from a foreign nation. Bathsheba got pregnant by a man she wasn't married to. They were not the perfect examples you would want to associate with a holy Saviour. I suspect this was no coincidence, but a deliberate act by God to show us that he can use imperfect women for his perfect purpose, irrespective of their pasts.

God's love is so overwhelming! The thing about God is that he is complete and absolute in love, with or without your own contribution to the equation. He doesn't love you any less when you are disobedient. The beautiful thing, however, is that when you experience his overwhelming love, you gain the ability to love him back in return. Even our failings and unfaithfulness fade into insignificance in the light of God's overwhelming love:

> The Lord is compassionate and merciful,
> slow to get angry and filled with unfailing love.
> He will not constantly accuse us,
> nor remain angry forever,
> He does not punish us for all our sins;
> he does not deal harshly with us, as we deserve.
> For his unfailing love toward those who fear him
> is as great as the height of the heavens above the
> earth (Psalm 103:8-11).

That is how forgiving and redeeming God's love is towards us. That is the same love he is extending to you today, waiting for you to accept and embrace it. So rather than trying so hard to appease God and pay for past sins, confess them to him and accept his forgiveness. He loves you just as you are. He still has plans for you greater than your imagination can hold.

INVITING GOD IN

God wants to be your Friend, Father, and Lover. His love is more than what any human can offer, and he desires intimacy with you. He wants to be the first and most significant person in your life.

You can begin an intimate relationship with God today by taking a few minutes right now to talk to him and tell him how you feel and renew your commitment to him. You will be amazed at what an adventure it is to have God as your friend. Would you take a plunge and choose to have an intimate love relationship with God?

I want to share the steps I took to start this journey of intimacy with God when I said a prayer inviting him into my life. It looked so simple, even for a child of eight years old, and I didn't quite understand the import of that prayer. But heaven took it into account. What counts is that you say it from a genuine heart.

HE IS EAGERLY HOPING YOU WILL RESPOND TO HIS OFFER OF LOVE.

Just use the "ABC" to guide your prayer:

A: Acknowledge that you're a sinner. Our good deeds can't meet the standards of a holy God. What's more, sin is not only an act that you do, but a nature we were all born into. As humans, we are naturally selfish and rebellious. We harm others and ourselves, breaking our relationships and shaming our Creator. Admitting we have hurt God is the first step.

B: Believe in the Lord Jesus Christ. As we talked about earlier, Jesus's death on the cross made a way for our sins to be forgiven, our relationship with God to be restored, and our shame to be removed.

C: Confess him as your Lord and Saviour. Tell Jesus that you trust him to rescue you from your destructive path and that you want him to have control of your life instead. Invite him to rule as God. Ask him for the new and eternal life that he has won through his death and resurrection – and he will give it to you freely!

It's possible you have made this decision in the past, but you still don't feel a depth of intimacy with God, or you seem to have lost the spark. If so, I want you to take a few minutes now to have a conversation with God in your own words. Remember, it's your Father, Lover, and Friend that you're talking to, so feel free to express yourself to him with genuine desire and expectation. God is not far off so that you need to travel to him; he is right where you are. You will discover that much more than you want to find him, he is trying to reach you! He is eagerly hoping you will respond to his offer of love.

DEEPENING OUR INTIMACY WITH GOD

Like any relationship, our relationship and intimacy with God grows as we spend time together and invest in it. So once we've made that initial commitment, we need to continue to cultivate intimacy with him.

Desire to be close to God. The first step to cultivating a relationship with God is a desire to know him. Nothing breeds knowledge more than curiosity. Perhaps you have tried making friends with people only for them to snub you, so you felt burned and withdrew. Unlike them, God is friendly and not snobbish. He will honour our desire to be close to him because he desires to be close to us more than we want to be to him. As James 4:8 says, "Come close to God, and God will come close to you."

Spend time with God. Nothing fosters intimacy more than spending quality time with someone whom you wish to be close to. Life is fast-paced and 24 hours hardly seems enough, so we need to deliberately carve out time to communicate with God. We make time to talk to God in prayer and listen to hear what he might have to say back. It helps to build it into our routines every day, preferably the first thing when you wake up and the last thing before going to bed. It's not about the length of time as much as it is the consistency.

I talk to God in the course of my day, too, during my commute, at work, at lunch, or when I'm in a difficult situation. You can talk to God in your thoughts rather than aloud, and you'll be surprised how he talks back to you by putting thoughts in your mind and planting ideas about how to navigate your day.

Another way to cultivate intimacy with God is to spend longer time with him when I'm more available, such as during the weekend. I have found at times that I need to trim down other activities such as chatting, watching movies, or sleeping in. But we create time for people we love, even if it means trading off on other things.

Study the Bible. The way to learn more about a subject matter is to read about it. That's why when a lecturer teaches us the basics of a subject, they still refer us to the textbook for further study. It is the same thing with getting to know God better. We can't rely only on what we're taught in church or from preaching online. We have to dig into the Bible with a lot of curiosity. As we open up our hearts and our Bibles, we will find that we understand God's Word and nature better. The Holy Spirit who inspired the Scripture will expound it to us, as though we were sitting with the author of a book as he explains his thoughts behind each section.

Meditate on God's Word. Scripture comes alive when we memorize it, think deeply on it, and recite it to ourselves. That is the act of meditation. We tend to quickly forget what we read, but memorizing and going over the words again keeps them fresh in our minds. We also receive new revelations, as if we are interacting with God and he is speaking directly to us. This is because the Word of God is actually alive, and we can interact with it.

Stay connected to other believers. I'm amazed at the bond people create over sports. Being around sports lovers inspires great love for the sport in you, helps you to know more about the sport, keeps you abreast of happenings in the clubs where you pledge allegiance, and gives a sense of belonging and kinship. It is similar to staying connected with other people who are genuinely seeking to be close to God. They inspire us to be close to God, extend fellowship to us, share their knowledge of God, and remind us that we belong to the family of God on earth.

THREE WORDS

As you spend time with God and deepen your relationship with him, I pray that you experience his love in fresh, real ways that you could never have imagined.

Some years ago, things looked quite good on the outside, but inside I felt a heavy weight of dissatisfaction. I felt a temporary sense of relief after I resigned from my job. But two years down the line, I realized the weight still had not fully lifted. Confused and lacking peace, I felt an urgent need to seek God's face for direction for my life. I decided to take some days off to go somewhere quiet where I could spend time alone in prayer.

I was expecting some massive revelation and blueprint for the next phase of my life, especially for my business. After seven days of praying and fasting, to my shock and even disappointment, the only thing I heard distinctly was three words: "I LOVE YOU."

I shared this experience with my friend when I got back. She gave me an incredulous look. "Are you serious? You spent seven days praying and all he told you was that he loves you? Did you let him know you were not joking, that you were paying hotel bills?"

> **YOU ARE LOVED BEYOND WHAT YOU CAN EVER IMAGINE.**

I laughed out loud. But I guess it was very important that the foundation of knowing God's love which passes all understanding was laid in my heart. That week I had heard it over and over and over! I heard it so loud and clear that it broke me. I started to repent for rejecting God's love and not trusting him enough. The revelation of God's love for me was so real that I would sit for hours and just cry.

I came away from those seven days with less clarity about the future than I would have liked, but so assured of and immersed in God's love. It was, for me, the beginning of a deeper intimacy with God. It emboldened me. From then on, I have learned to relate with God not just as a Father and friend but also as a lover.

I hope that if you get nothing else from this book, that message resonates deep down into your soul. God is saying: "I LOVE YOU." He will be there for you no matter who else comes in and out of your life. He is your Father, who gave you life, who gently guides you by the hand, and who holds you close. He is your friend who cares about every detail of your life and is always ready to pick up your calls. He is the ultimate lover of your soul who fills a void no one else can fill. You are loved beyond what you can ever imagine.

Happily Ever After Starts Here

Reflections

- How do you see God? What do you think has influenced your picture of God the most?

_____
_____
_____
_____

- How has your relationship with your biological father or father figures affected your relationship with God?

_____
_____
_____
_____

- What does God's love mean to you?

_____
_____
_____

- How would you describe your relationship with God right now?

_____
_____
_____
_____

- What do you wish your relationship with God was like?

_____
_____
_____
_____

Exercise

- Take a moment to talk to God as if he were right next to you, because he is. You don't need to talk out loud, but you can. Be open and sincere, and tell him how you feel. You don't need to be formal or try to make a good impression. Ask God to speak to you and invite him to be part of your week.

- In the course of this week, listen and look out consciously for how he will reply or what he would like to say to you. It could be through a convincing thought in your mind, a verse from the Bible, a conversation with other people, or online content that brings a lot of conviction and clarity. Note these down in a journal.

What the Bible says about God's love for you

"I have loved you, my people, with an everlasting love. With unfailing love, I have drawn you to myself" (Jeremiah 31:3).

Thrive Right Where You Are!

At recent training, I chatted with two other ladies at my table while we waited for the facilitator to arrive. "I'm married," said the first. Her voice exuded the telltale excitement of a newlywed. She directed her stare at me. "How about you?"

"Well, I'm happily single," I replied with a smile.

"And I," said the third lady, "am happily getting a divorce."

We all burst out laughing. As the three of us realized, we can choose happiness and contentment regardless of our marital status.

When I first realized I was going to be a *princess* at that bridal shower 12 years ago, singleness seemed like a sentence that banished you into a life of total misery and doom. But I've since learned that singleness isn't synonymous to sadness. As we wrap up our time together, I want to leave you with a final encouragement to pursue joy!

WHY PUT HAPPINESS ON HOLD?

A few months or years before my friends approached 40, I would ask them what they wanted or planned to do to celebrate their 40th birthday. It was not unusual that my single friends would often respond with something like, "I'll be in my husband's house" or "I'll go on vacation with my husband to Maldives or the USA."

Well, you might not be surprised to learn that their wishes didn't happen. I understand that hardly any lady wants to be 40 and single, but why are you waiting for a husband to live happily ever after? As single ladies, should we put happiness on hold until we find marital bliss?

I love how Jackie talks about maximizing the single life: "As African women, we're trained to be subservient, to apologize for our strength and for wanting things. I say, no, don't do that. God created you beautifully and he made you wonderful. The right person will enhance that in you. Don't dim your light. You don't know who you will marry, what your relationship will end up being, what you will have to be engaged in as a married couple. What you do know is what you have now.

"So, if you want to travel, travel. You want to study? Study. Have the fullest life you possibly can. Experiment to make the changes, pivot where you have to, but figure yourself out. Learn what you like to do, what you love doing, what you don't like doing."

WHAT DO YOU DO FOR FUN?

"What do you do for fun?" Simple as this question is, in recent times, whenever I'm asked this question, I go blank. What a contrast to my younger self!

In my 20s, it was "one week, one party". Trust me, as a Nigerian, I wasn't in short supply of social events to attend. You would hardly ever find me at home on a weekend. If there were no activities, I created one. I joined a dance class, took swimming lessons, attended poetry or book readings, went on boat rides, travelled for fun, or organized hangouts and sleepovers with friends. Now, I realize I'm not in the same life stage as I was back then. But remembering that time has made me resolve to rediscover what brings me joy – and pursue it!

And so should you! Find ways to celebrate accomplishments and special occasions. Make birthday plans that don't require a husband. You could do a photoshoot, give yourself a spa treat, buy yourself a gift, or go on a trip if you can afford it. Just do something special and different for yourself. If you actually are in your husband's house at that time, that's great too.

God has put in you the ability to have fun and given you things to enjoy right now. Life doubtless comes with its own challenges, but you can choose to thrive through it. The words of the preacher in Ecclesiastes 8:15 sums it up nicely:

> So I recommend having fun, because there is nothing better for people in this world than to eat, drink, and enjoy life. That way they will experience some happiness along with all the hard work God gives them under the sun.

So, let's rediscover ourselves. Do you want to travel more? Meet new people? Learn to speak a new language, draw, bake, or paint? Do you need to learn to be grateful, to rest your body, to communicate during conflict, or to sustain your relationships?

Perhaps having a full single life means making adjustments to your habits, routines, and lifestyle. We must also be good to our bodies so it can be good to us in return and serve us longer and better. Learn the rhythm of your body, go for medical check-ups – and not just when you're about to drop (a lesson I've had to learn myself!). Find the right diet for you and stick to it. Exercise. Use the right multivitamins. Get some of that sunshine Africa is blessed with! Spend your time wisely and build habits that will oil the wheel of the changes you are seeking.

BUILD HABITS THAT OIL THE WHEEL OF THE CHANGES YOU SEEK.

Let's enjoy life and rich relationships in our singlehood. God has created us to have deep relationships – it is not good for humans to be alone. The ladies I interviewed have great support systems, be they family, friends, mentors, and circles of accountability. We need other people to become all we're made for. Isn't it great to know that as a child of God, you can have a robust life, irrespective of your marital status? You will always belong in his family.

The single ladies I have seen achieving their purpose have deep, intimate relationships with God. Everything they are and have achieved is an outflow of their walk with God. God is at the centre of their lives holding all the different parts together. They are women of faith, full of trust, always ready to go on the next adventure of faith with God, irrespective of the price to be paid.

It's never too late to invest in your relationship with God. It doesn't matter how badly life has served you or how much you've messed up. God is a God of redemption. If you find yourself overwhelmed by this journey of growing and becoming, you can trust God entirely and rely on him (Proverbs 3:5-6).

I'm so sure that when we do good and take delight in him, we can trust him to give us his best. Psalm 37:3-7 reminds us to trust that "he will give you your heart's desires . . . he will help you . . . Be still in the presence of the Lord, and wait patiently for him to act." God can bring you into a new season and a secure place where you can start to blossom and live the best version of your life that is possible.

Pursue purpose. You don't have to wait to be married to start living out your potential. God has a work for you to do as a piece of the puzzle in his grander scheme of things. Find your life's assignment. Do work that gives you joy and satisfaction, blesses other people, and gives glory to God.

Every time I read the Epistles, I am awed by Paul's life and how much work he did for the kingdom of God. Like Jesus, thousands of years after his death, his words are still relevant, even in this technology-forward world. I can't help but imagine if he would have made such an enormous impact had he been married.

That's what I love about the women I interviewed for this book. They are not sitting on their hands, waiting for a man to arrive before they start to do the work they were born to do. They know that, like my pastor says, "You're too small to be the purpose of your own life." So their lives are bigger than themselves.

They are busy pursuing their God-given assignments and impacting their world. They are audacious in their dreams. They continue to grow and build their competences, not just because of financial gains or accomplishments, but because they need to grow in their capacities to be able to help others grow. That's why their passion is contagious.

DO WORK THAT GIVES YOU JOY AND SATISFACTION.

Are their lives perfect? No. They, too, have their moments of being down, broke, and dependent on others for their sustenance. They have felt unworthy or afraid of what the future holds. Some have had their lives in danger, suffered heartbreak and betrayal, and had no place to call home. But they inspire us to see what God can do with us if we cooperate with him and decide to live our lives to the fullest, right where we are.

It was so enlightening to hear from people like Jackie and Eugenia that we're not walking this path alone. Other unmarried women are happy and fulfilled – and it's possible even if marriage never happens. I must confess that after this series of interviews, I've been inspired to pick up my dreams again.

STEPPING INTO HAPPILY EVER AFTER

It's not just the single ladies I spoke to that have awesome stories. I know the same God is doing something great in you. I want to acknowledge the transformation he is making, helping you to step into his grand design for your life, even as a single lady. I hope this book has encouraged you to take your place in God's kingdom and to live a rich, enjoyable, and fulfilled life.

Yes, we can change the stereotype about the mature single lady having a forlorn disposition. We can start to remove the cap society has placed on us about what we're capable of becoming. We can evolve from our larvae state and the place of hibernating into that beautiful butterfly ready to fly; we can add colour to an already gloomy world.

Trust God for the best of everything he wants for you. Step into the fullness of who God has made you and live this life you've been given to the fullest! Happily ever after doesn't have to wait until you're married . . . it starts here and now!

Happily Ever After Starts Here

Reflections

- What were the activities you enjoyed while you were younger? What would you like to do for fun now?

_____

_____

_____

- What are some things you might be holding back from doing until a husband comes along?

_____

_____

_____

- What is stopping you from pursuing those goals, changes, or things that bring you joy now?

_____

_____

_____

Exercise

- Have you been conditioned to feel that you don't deserve or haven't earned the right to be happy until you're married? What would a picture of living your best life look like? What will you start doing from now to make this picture a reality?

_____

_____

_____

_____

_____

_____

_____

_____

_____

_____

- Take time this week to do something just for the frivolity of it, rather than for actual results or returns. It could be a hobby, celebrating yourself, dining out, or something you love and haven't done for a long time. Enjoy the moment!

What the Bible says about your happily ever after

The way of the righteous is like the first gleam of dawn, which shines ever brighter until the full light of day (Proverbs 4:18).

About the Author

Bookie Adekanye has not only navigated the challenges that come with being a single lady into her 40s in an African society, but she has also helped many other single women thrive by creating a community that fosters peer support and safe spaces for them. Her passion is to see people live happy and purposeful lives, irrespective of their status and station in life. With her Facebook series the "Diary of a Mature Single Lady" under the pseudonym Hadassah, Bookie's signature humor and honesty have endeared her to readers. Bookie is a certified Christian counsellor, writer, teacher, entrepreneur, travel enthusiast, lover of nature, and mentor to young people. She currently lives in Ontario, Canada.

You can connect with Bookie through her website: **www.happilywheneverafter.com**.

Acknowledgements

The journey to writing this book began well over a decade ago. Many people have walked along this path with me.

To them, I am greatly indebted.

Firstly, I'd like to thank my family: My mom, who gave me the gift of storytelling. My dad, whose unconventional role as a man, father, and head of the family has shaped my worldview and formed a positive frame of reference for me. My siblings who are ever so supportive, even as I continue to choose paths that are not easily explainable. I have been blessed to have a family that does not put me under pressure for not being married. This is quite rare and atypical given the backdrop of the African society in which we exist, and I don't take this for granted.

I would be remiss if I forgot to acknowledge the people who have been an active part of my journey as an author: Mobolaji Banjo, who was the first person to open my eyes to the intrinsic value in my writing; Seun Akisanmi, who took it upon himself to compile my posts on Facebook because he believed they needed to be published; and Edmund Jones who said to me, "Bookie, write something, anything, and I'll get you a publisher." I am also grateful to Modupe Ehirim. It was through her that I found the opportunity of having my book published by Oasis International.

I am also grateful to everyone who shared valuable input for this book. There is an adage that says "it takes all the fingers on a hand to beat one's chest in a show of confidence." Pastor Nike Wilhems shared great insight into marriage culture through African lenses. In the course of writing this book, I interviewed several women from different backgrounds at different stages of life. It is their wisdom, rich perspectives, lived experience, and expert opinions that have been woven into the threads of this book to give it a richer and more robust outlook than I would have single-handedly been able to put together. To these women, I say "Thank you for your vulnerability in sharing your inspiring stories with us. My life has been greatly enriched by you, as I'm sure the lives of other women who read this book will be."

To everyone who has cheered me on along this journey, those who gave great reviews, comments, and feedback on the first version of the book: you are the reason why we have a new and better version of the book *Happily Whenever After*. Thank you!

Lastly, I'd like to say a big thank you to Hannah Rasmussen, my editor for all her hard work and dedication. It was a lot of hard work, and several rounds of iteration to get this book out. "Hey, Hannah, we finally have a book!"

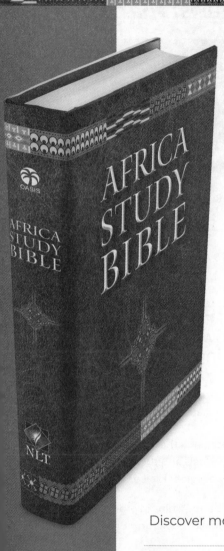